TRUJILLO:
THE LAST
CAESAR

TRUJILLO:
THE LAST
CAESAR

ARTURO R. ESPAILLAT

HENRY REGNERY COMPANY
CHICAGO · 1963

Contents

To the Reader

I am aware that this book won't make pretty reading. I also realize that I tend to make light of violence and sudden death. The fact is, friends, those things are almost as common in your world as in mine. It is only that in the northern democracies, the law of the jungle less openly prevails. I have had to live and work by that law for so many years that I no longer bother to pretend that it doesn't exist.

Prologue

AGAIN I found myself staring, half-hypnotized, into the bright overhead light. When are they going to turn the damn thing off, I wondered. Wearily, I straightened up in my chair and glanced at the guard. As always, he was staring at me through the bars of my cell. His face was expressionless.

I still don't know why I had been jailed. And by Ramfis, by my good friend Gen. Rafael Leonidas Trujillo, Jr., son of the man—now dead—whom I had served for almost 20 years. Oh, well, I shrugged, it's not unusual for security chiefs to end up behind bars. It seems to be a sort of occupational hazard.

He'll shoot me, I told myself for the thousandth time. He'll sure as hell have me shot. Ramfis is smart enough to know that he can't just turn me loose after this. But all I could do was wait. I recalled a phrase I had learned at the beginning of my plebe year at West Point. "Mister," the upperclassman had said as he braced me in the hall, "when rape is inevitable, relax and enjoy it." I smiled at the memory and began to relax.

The date was June 22, 1961, some three weeks after the assassination of Generalissimo Rafael Leonidas Trujillo, last of the old-style Caribbean strongmen. And yet, including Trujillo in that category is not quite accurate. Trujillo was unique.

No single ruler of modern times has held the absolute power that Trujillo wielded over his three million people for 31 years. His rule was as absolute as that of any Roman emperor. I thought of Caligula, the mad Caesar. Caligula once appointed a horse to be consul of Rome. Trujillo certainly could have announced that a horse was to be named president of the Dominican Republic, and Dominicans would have accepted it. But, whatever else he was, Trujillo was no madman.

But what *was* he? I pondered that question as I sprawled in my chair, my eyes shut tight against the light flooding my cell. What had been Trujillo's motivations? What "made him tick?" Even I, one of his closest aides, was not sure. The Old Man was an extraordinary and complex being.

I doubt that Trujillo had ever read Machiavelli. I had. In Machiavelli's "The Prince" I had found the key to many of Trujillo's own political actions and precepts. Machiavelli advised that if a ruler had to choose between being loved and being feared he should choose the latter, although he should avoid being hated. Trujillo succeeded in making himself both loved and feared.

His guiding precept was "Do it to others before they can do it to you." He relied on himself alone—on his guns, his power, his capabilities. And they were such that his awed subjects came to look upon Trujillo as a sort of superhuman force.

It was this very success which doomed him. As Machiavelli points out, circumstances change and the same qualities which had once brought victory can eventually produce defeat; human nature is such that powerful men find it impossible to adjust themselves to the change. That had been the case with Trujillo.

The ideological and social revolutions which swept the world after World War II also swirled around the Dominican Republic. Trujillo's non-ideological dictatorship stood increasingly alone. The Old Man became a living anachronism. The wonder is that he lasted so long, for the other old-style dictatorships, one by one, were being swept away.

In vain, Trujillo boasted of the material progress he had brought to his country, of the roads, schools, highways, bridges he had built. The answer came back that they had been built at too high a price in human blood and dignity.

His power, which had once extended throughout the Caribbean and into the United States, dwindled. The swarm of Washington officials he had bribed fell silent. Pressure mounted against him, both from Communism and from forces inside the United States. The Catholic Church turned against him. Still he fought on. Internally, police suppression became ever more barbaric. It was not that Trujillo would not change. He could not. He continued believing in guns right up to the time he was cut down by them. By then, he had outlived all usefulness, even to himself.

Nevertheless, his enemies couldn't overthrow Trujillo. They had to kill him. I took some satisfaction in that fact. Not that it mattered now, I thought, looking again at the bars and the silent guard. Anyway, I still had enough of a sense of humor to appreciate the irony of my situation.

When Trujillo was killed, I had held the country together until the crown prince, Ramfis, returned from a spree in Europe. A few weeks later Ramfis clapped me into one of the cell blocks of the Military Intelligence Service.

I remain neither ashamed nor regretful of my years as an intelligence officer. I earned my *nom de guerre* "Navajita"—The Blade—not because I was guilty of any atrocities. The name stemmed from my tendency to plunge straight to the heart of any problem or situation. I believed in direct, simple action. However, there is not a single Dominican who has or can come forward to prove that I caused him to be tortured. Nor can any Dominican family charge that one of its members died at my hands or at my orders.

I had an answer for any worried relatives who came to my office to inquire about a relative arrested by the Security Police. "If he has done nothing, he will be released before the third day." That was my standard operating procedure. The suspect would either be released or would face open trial.

And now it was my turn. I was being held incommunicado and there was not the slightest chance of receiving trial.

Not that I was outraged by this breach of my "civil rights." I had always considered words like "human rights" to be something invented by liberals to hinder my operations. An old leopard like me does not change his spots. The spots merely lose their luster and fade. However, I had found that being in solitary confinement was not conducive to continuing one's enthusiasm for dictatorship.

Ramfis tricked me into my present predicament. A Maj. Octavio Balcazar, chief of Ramfis' personal Secret Police, had come to see me at army headquarters.

"General," he said, "General Trujillo, Jr. wants to see you in my office." Balcazar's office was located in the secret police prison. Ramfis was not there when we arrived. We waited for a few minutes in Balcazar's office. Then he got a phone call. "I have to leave for a few minutes," he told me, "but please wait here for the General."

Balcazar walked out. Seven men walked in. They asked me if I would mind waiting in "the little room down the hall." I did mind, I told them, but those seven pistols they were pointing at me were very persuasive.

My "little room" was a cell with an office chair but no bed. I didn't yet know it, but I was going to get the "no-sleep treatment." That was something new in the Dominican Republic. Ramfis had read about it while he was in Paris and I remember he had once discussed the technique. Ramfis always wanted to keep up with the times.

I spent the night trying to figure out why I had been

jailed. The light had been left on, but I didn't pay much attention to it. I was brought an excellent breakfast. That was followed by an equally good lunch and dinner. All during the treatment I was well fed. That is part of the no-sleep technique. The stronger one is physically, the more impact the treatment has on the mind. The process lasts longer and is more thorough when the prisoner is well-fed.

That night I managed to doze for a few minutes. But the tension and the powerful light made real sleep impossible.

Next morning I was groggy. Tonight, I told myself, I am going to sleep, light or no light. But that evening the comfortable office chair was replaced by a straight-backed chair. My guards told me they had strict orders that I was not to sleep.

A day later and my guards could keep me awake only by beating me with sticks. Two days of near-delirium passed. Then the guards, all of whom I knew personally, began to relax their vigilance just a bit. From time to time they let me doze—if I sat on that straight-back chair, my face to the glaring light.

The guards became more lax as time passed. I was permitted to doze for about 15 minutes at a time. But never was I able to manage more than an hour's sleep a day. It was just not enough. The walls began to shimmy and I would fall face forward out of my chair when the floor suddenly seemed to dissolve. Strange monsters began to slither through the room.

I couldn't coordinate my movements and speech. My mental processes were short-circuited. I could no longer think, only feel in a vague sort of way. The monsters grew larger and my whole cell faded into a shimmering fog. And then I blacked out completely.

I awoke on a cot somebody had placed in my cell. A

young lieutenant, seated in my chair, was watching me. He arose and told me that I was free on Ramfis' order. I was driven to my home. A few days later I went into exile.

Why was I imprisoned? I assume that Ramfis considered me a potential competitor for power. Why was I freed? Perhaps my death would have been difficult to explain to the other army officers.

Some four months later, Ramfis and his relatives fled into exile. It was the end of the Dominican Republic's so-called Era of Trujillo, the collapse of one of the most publicized and reviled dictatorships in Latin American history. Until now, however, the real story behind the Era of Trujillo—its last, brutal decade—has never been told.

TRUJILLO:
THE LAST
CAESAR

1

End of the Era

ONE Sunday morning in January, 1960, Dominicans filed silently into their churches and were hit by a clerical bombshell. A pastoral letter denouncing Trujillo was read in every Catholic Church in the republic. The letter, signed by all the country's bishops, was read at each successive Mass that Sunday. Needless to say, attendance at the later Masses broke all records.

"This is incredible," I heard one government official comment. "After all that Trujillo has done for the Church!"

"Not only that," his friend shot back, "this after all that the Church has done for Trujillo!"

Both remarks characterized Trujillo's years-long relationship with the Catholic Church. From the beginning, Trujillo had ardently wooed the Church. He gave huge subsidies, built scores of churches, established Catholic schools, convents and monasteries. In return, the Church hierarchy heaped praise and honors on Trujillo. In 1936, the Vatican decorated Trujillo with the highest category of the Order of St. Gregory the Great, the Church's highest honor.

More practically, from Trujillo's point of view, Dominicans became accustomed to hearing his praises sung from the pulpit and in public announcements by the Church hierarchy. As a matter of fact, I can recall an election rally at which the most passionately pro-Trujillo speaker was Monsignor Perez Sanchez. He was at that time a member of Trujillo's rubberstamp congress.

1

The high point of the Old Man's honeymoon with the
Church came in 1954. That was the year Trujillo travelled
to Rome to sign a Concordat with the Pope, officially con-
firming the Church's privileged position in the Dominican
Republic. For himself, Trujillo was granted an annulment
of his first marriage, thereby enabling him to go through a
religious marriage ceremony with his second wife.

Even I was honored. I had accompanied the Old Man
as chief of his escort and was decorated with the Order
of St. Gregory in one of the lesser categories. A few years
later I was able to reciprocate. As New York Consul General I attended a ceremony in St. Patrick's Cathedral and
decorated Cardinal Spellman with the Dominican Republic's highest decoration.

On another occasion, Church prelates from all over the
world—including Cardinal Spellman and Ecuadorian Car-
dinal de la Torre—flocked to Ciudad Trujillo to attend the
International Congress of Catholic Culture for World
Peace. The two princes of the church were housed in the
National Palace as Trujillo's personal guests.

I am certainly not condemning the hierarchy's former
support of Trujillo. From its point of view, the Old Man
did great things for the Church. (The Church was, in fact,
only a minor institution in our country until Trujillo threw
his weight behind it.) Undoubtedly, another reason was
the Old Man's uncompromising anti-Communism. He
worked hard at being the "First Anti-Communist of the
Americas." Under Trujillo, Communism simply didn't exist in the Dominican Republic. Moreover, the Old Man
was always ready to support anti-Communist leaders any-
where in the Caribbean.

For his part, Trujillo knew from the beginning that
bringing the Church under his influence would aid in his
consolidation of power. He felt that he could survive only
by controlling or neutralizing *all* sources of political power.
And the Church represented a cohesive, if minor, power
bloc.

That power suddenly turned on him in January, 1960. The rupture was not gradual. There were no preliminaries, no advance warning. The pastoral letter hit Trujillo like a bolt from heaven. However, there may have been one hint that the Church had seen the handwriting on Trujillo's wall when the Papal Nuncio, an ardent *trujillista,* was suddenly replaced by a prelate with far more independent views.

The new Papal Nuncio summoned the five bishops of the Dominican Republic. He laid it on the line: the Church could no longer be identified with Trujillo. There could be no compromise, no middle way. The results were dramatic

It was the first time I had ever seen the Old Man rattled. The rest of the official family was in a state of shock. There was a ceremony that Sunday evening at the Cattle Fair. Normally a festive affair, that night it was more like a funeral.

The pastoral letter was only a link—a vitally important one—in a violent chain reaction which was eventually to destroy the regime. Trujillo was trapped in a vicious circle.

The June, 1959 invasions of the Dominican Republic, openly sponsored by Cuba and Venezuela, had inspired the birth of an underground, calling itself the 14th of June Movement. This group—which also received the tacit support of Cuba and Venezuela—was the only major, well-organized anti-Trujillo organization to operate in the Dominican Republic. Cells sprang up throughout the country. Membership numbered in the hundreds.

Soon, a massive assassination plot against Trujillo was discovered, just prior to its execution. This produced an even more sweeping wave of brutal police repression, as well as the January pastoral letter denouncing that brutality. Suddenly, Trujillo was being belted from every direction. He struck back wildly. Repression mounted; so did internal and external counter-pressures.

Trujillo found himself fighting on wide-ranging fronts:

religious, political, economic and subversive. His response
to conspiracy was, of course, direct: imprisonment, torture
and death. On the political front, Trujillo went through
the motions of reforming the regime (as well as dispatch-
ing emissaries to Washington to collect the political debts
owed him by the politicians he had bribed—but now they
wanted no part of him).

The Old Man never did really figure out how to cope
with his Church problem. His aides were also confused and
divided. Some were of the opinion that the Church issue
should be ignored. Others urged drastic retaliation.

But, as usual, Trujillo made his own decisions. Once
he had got a grip on himself, the Old Man studied the
situation. Three of the five bishops and most of the Catholic clergymen in the republic were foreigners, and thus
had no relatives Trujillo could use as hostages.

When he had reached his decision, Trujillo acted. He
took no drastic steps. He did not even cut off the subsidies,
an act which would have crippled Church activities in the
Dominican Republic. For a while the Old Man contem-
plated the expulsion of the foreign clergy. He decided
against it. No overt measures were taken against the
Church.

Instead, Trujillo launched an unofficial campaign of harassment. Publicly, Trujillo piously condemned the campaign to discredit the clergy. Privately, the Old Man
worked feverishly to embarrass and undermine hostile prelates.

The principal target was the Papal Nuncio. Trujillo held
him responsible for all the trouble. Harassment of the Nuncio was climaxed with what was probably the most ludicrous hoax ever perpetrated by a chief of state.

The Old Man had heard that the Nuncio had sent out
invitations to a small noon-hour reception to be held at the
Nunciatura a few days hence. On the morning of the scheduled reception, messengers bearing invitations fanned

throughout the city. Every top government official, plus many in the lower echelons, received an invitation. It was also broadly hinted that attendance was compulsory, since Trujillo himself would attend.

Sure enough, promptly at noon, the Old Man turned up at the Nunciatura, invitation in hand. The Nuncio, forewarned, had locked the building and gone into hiding. Trujillo pretended to be puzzled, then calmly observed that there must have been a slight mix-up. By this time, traffic for blocks around the building was jammed by hundreds of other "guests" earnestly trying to reach the reception. This affair was too much for the Nuncio. He left the country next day and never returned.

But the flight of the Nuncio solved nothing. Other powerful forces were now arrayed against him. The Trujillo regime began to be bombarded by one political bombshell after another. This series of setbacks has been succinctly described by Norman Gall, a reporter for the San Juan *Star*. In the *New Republic* magazine of April 13, 1963, Gall told "How Trujillo Died":

"1960 was a bad year for the Dominican Republic. The economy was in the dumps. The country was in disgrace internationally as a result of Trujillo's backing of a plot against the life of Venezuelan President Romulo Betancourt. In June, a car full of explosives blew up alongside Betancourt's automobile during a Caracas Armed Forces Day procession, wounding the president and killing two others. A Venezuelan naval officer later admitted that the elaborate bomb was prepared in the Dominican Republic, presumably as an act of retaliation against Venezuela for having asked the OAS in February, 1960, to censure Trujillo for 'flagrant violation of human rights.'

"In August that same year, the Organization of American States did censure the Dominican Republic, and the U.S. and several Latin American nations thereupon suspended diplomatic relations with the Trujillo regime, though Washington kept a consulate in Ciudad Trujillo to protect its commercial interests.

"This was one of the stormiest periods of Trujillo's 31-year rule. On June 14, 1959, the Dominican Republic's southern coast had been invaded by Cuba-based Dominican exiles. They were wiped out, but then Trujillo uncovered a plot to kill him, only 24 hours before it was to be carried out on January 21, 1960. Mass purges, arrests and some killings followed. Tensions within the regime mounted rapidly, as did its Byzantine-style ruler's greed. Assuming the presidency of the Dominican Central Bank, the dictator forced exporters, as part of an 'austerity' program, to deposit with the bank half of their dollar earnings, which soon found their way into Trujillo's accounts abroad."

Gall made two errors in the foregoing paragraph. First, the invaders did not land on the southern coast. Second, Trujillo did not bank money abroad during his last years. He had not the slightest intention of fleeing the country. He knew that he was fighting for his political—and physical—life, and actually ploughed back into the Dominican economy several million dollars deposited with the Royal Bank of Canada.

Gall continues:

"During this time, Trujillo was completing an intensive drive, begun in the mid-1950's with the purchase of the Haina complex of sugar mills and lands in the southern part of the republic, to expand sugar production and appropriate more and more of it to himself. He went so far as to deprive thousands of peasant families of their squatters' settlements, forcing them to sell their cattle and work as sugar peons. It had been hoped, of course, that the Dominican Republic would get a generous share of the U.S. sugar quota previously allotted to Cuba. An intensive Washington lobbying campaign was carried on to this end, largely through the Dominican Consul General to Washington, Marco A. Pena. In the late summer of 1960, Congress did raise the Dominican allotment from 27,000 tons to 250,000 tons, but President Eisenhower slapped a punitive excise tax on it in September, after the OAS ministerial conference voted economic sanctions against the Trujillo regime and a break of diplomatic relations."

Relations between the U.S. Ambassador and Trujillo had been virtually suspended months before the formal break. Throughout 1960 the Old Man was bombarded by a mounting publicity campaign and the ambassador, Joseph Farland, a political appointee, went underground for the duration. This was on orders, Trujillo learned from his spies in the American Embassy. The State Department clipped all the news stories and forwarded them to Farland with instructions to stay out of the line of fire.

Not surprisingly, it was Farland's own embassy staff which was generating most of the stories. Some American correspondents would come down and do little more than shuttle back and forth between the Hotel Embajador and the Embassy, and send out bloodcurdling copy.

As time passed, an interesting phenomenon became apparent; the more Fidel Castro clobbered Washington, the more Washington clobbered Trujillo. In a sense, Fidel can be said to have carried out his promise to destroy the Dominican dictatorship: Castro goaded Washington to such an extent that the State Department did it for him.

The first hint that Washington would use force against Trujillo, if not against Castro, came in the summer of 1960. It was a curiously inane episode.

A U.S. Embassy intelligence officer called the Palace and said it was urgent that he talk secretly with Trujillo. He was told to meet with one of the Old Man's aides.

The Embassy official came to the Palace and told an odd story. He had come, he said, on his own. Such was his admiration of Trujillo that he was risking his career, the diplomat said solemnly, to warn of plans being made to oust the Chief. He had learned, our visitor continued, that Washington was planning to send the U.S. Navy against Trujillo if he didn't resign.

It was a transparent maneuver, a clumsy way to deliver a threat, and Trujillo treated it as such. A formal diplomatic protest was lodged. Washington ignored the protest, not even going through the motions of replacing the Embassy intelligence officer.

The second ultimatum was delivered a few months later. This one was presented—reluctantly, I think—by Trujillo's good friend William Pawley. The former U.S. ambassador to Peru and Brazil warned the Old Man that the time had come to call it quits. He suggested that Trujillo retire to Europe. Trujillo blew up.

"If I step out," he told Pawley, "I might as well turn my country over to Fidel Castro. It is obvious that the Communists know what they are doing, while your government does not."

Trujillo felt he had been betrayed, that his old friend had also turned against him. I don't think so. I think Pawley must have known that Trujillo would never submit. But I think Pawley also knew what was coming and was trying to save Trujillo's life.

In any event, Washington pulled out all stops when the Old Man rejected the second ultimatum. The U.S. government-controlled radio station on Swan Island, off the coast of Central America, took time off from attacking Castro to beam revolutionary propaganda at the Dominican Republic. U.S.-subsidized Cuban exile publications hurled invective. Economic sanctions dealt smashing blows at the Dominican economy.

But still Trujillo stood. He remained immensely powerful—and still immensely popular—in his own fortress-state. No revolution was remotely in sight.

So he had to be assassinated.

2

"Then Fall, Caesar"

INVESTIGATION of Trujillo's assassination began literally within minutes after his death. All but two of the conspirators were quickly captured or killed resisting arrest. And all who were captured quickly confessed. The pattern of the conspiracy was evident in less than a week. A very broad trail of evidence and testimony led directly to the curiously outsized U.S. Consulate in Ciudad Trujillo.

One version of the Consulate's activities was presented by *Chicago Daily News* Foreign Service reporter William McGaffin in Washington in a datelined article written shortly after the assassination:

"The possibility that a sudden and violent end might one day overtake Generalissimo Rafael Trujillo, the right-wing dictator of the Dominican Republic, is an event that U.S. officials anticipated and tried to prepare for.

"That is the real reason why the United States refused to go all the way in breaking relations with its Caribbean neighbor last August.

"A complete break was urged by some Organization of American States nations at a foreign ministers conference in San Jose, Costa Rica.

"The United States, however, successfully held out for the retention of consular relations while going along with the rupture of diplomatic relations.

"This means that while the United States pulled out its ambassador, it still had a consul general in the country. . . .

9

"The purpose behind the decision to keep Consul General Henry Dearborn and a staff of about 25 on station in the Dominican capital involved considerably more than the obvious advantages that might be realized from maintaining a listening post in a trouble spot. . . .

"It was hoped that if the United States continued to operate a consulate in the Dominican Republic, it would encourage the moderate elements in the country who were known to be opposed to the dictatorship. . . .

"Just how and what the U.S. consulate may have been able to do to keep the love of liberty and human values alive in this important group is something that no one here will discuss."

Norman Gall was more realistic in his *New Republic* account of "How Trujillo Died." Mr. McGaffin's "listening post" was the nerve center of a conspiracy which Trujillo himself would have admired. As Gall says:

"The assassination of the Dominican Republic's Rafael L. Trujillo was carried out with assistance from the U.S. Central Intelligence Agency. Arms for the May 30, 1961 slaying of the 69-year-old dictator on a lonely stretch of highway near his capital were smuggled by CIA into the country at the request of the assassins, according to highly qualified sources I interviewed in Santo Domingo shortly after the collapse of the Trujillo rule.

"The CIA began shipping guns to the Dominican Republic in late 1960. . . .

"The key link between the assassins and the CIA in the arms shipments was a long-time American civilian resident of Ciudad Trujillo . . . who operated a super market in a fashionable neighborhood where Trujillo also lived. . . . [He] was put under brief arrest after the killing but was later allowed to leave the country.

"The weapons were imported in small parts, to be assem-

bled later by the plotters, among the routine grocery shipments for the supermarket arriving regularly in the capital's
port. The gun-parts entered the Republic in specially
marked food cans, which were later turned over to the
conspirators."

Gall misstates the importance of the arms shipments to
the conspirators. The guns were delivered as he describes,
but the value of the weapons was almost entirely psychological. The conspirators had access to plenty of local fire-
power. Dominican officers, particularly of the higher ranks,
usually had virtual arsenals in their homes, weapons issued
or collected over the years. I myself had enough guns, from
pistols to machineguns, to have equipped a full infantry
platoon. The home of Gen. José René Roman Fernandez
was equally well stocked, as were those of other officers
who took part in the conspiracy.

But the arrival of weapons *from the Government of the
United States* was, for the plotters, tangible evidence that
the might of the United States was behind them. Without
that support there would simply have been no conspiracy.
Trujillo had put together a powerful political-military machine which could only have been destroyed by intervention from the outside world. And the State Department
had decreed: Trujillo must go.

"I'll retire only when I'm dead," the Old Man used to
tell me. He meant it. Power was the only reason for his
existence. Trujillo had no intention of following the example of the parade of ousted Latin American strongmen who
had passed through the Dominican Republic during their
flights. The forlorn faces of Rojas Pinilla, Perez Jimenez,
Peron and Batista were grim reminders of the fate of fallen
dictators.

Thus, as pressure mounted, Trujillo systematically entrenched himself deeper and deeper in his now-isolated
nation. He went on a grass-roots, political fence-mending

whirl which took him to every corner of the country. His magnetic appeal to the masses was still overwhelming. He oiled up the Trujillo machine and it functioned more smoothly than ever. Looking back, it still strikes me as almost unbelievable: assailed from all sides, under immense economic and political pressures, Trujillo held the Dominican Republic in an iron grip.

So there was only one way to get rid of the man. The final solution: he had to die. The plot began to take shape in the fall of 1960, shortly after the condemnation of the Trujillo regime at the Organization of American States conference in Costa Rica.

Masterminding the operation were two rather improbable conspirators. They were foreign service officers who had held posts in the U.S. Embassy until the rupture of relations, after which they had been transferred to the U.S. Consulate. The pair reminded me of the American comic strip characters Mutt and Jeff.

The taller of the two—let's call him Mutt—asked a mutual friend, a businessman named Manolin Alfaro, that I intercede with Trujillo on his behalf. Mutt wanted me to advise Trujillo that his, Mutt's, transfer to the Consulate should be accepted by the Dominican government. Mutt claimed that the transfer would help his career.

I did the opposite—Mutt was too eager. I strongly urged Trujillo not to accept the transfer. But the Old Man, always anxious to please Washington and, as always, immune to advice, was only too happy to comply with Mutt's request. It was typical that Trujillo would always be the last to admit that U.S. diplomats were knifing him in the back.

It was this same blind confidence that permitted the conspiracy to flower literally under his nose. Trujillo knew that Mutt and Jeff were in contact with oppositionists. It was fairly common knowledge in the government that the American's market was being used as a rendezvous by the two diplomats and oppositionists. But he and the diplomats were Americans. And Trujillo, always the ex-Marine, liked Americans.

The Dominicans who actually executed the conspiracy were an oddly mixed lot. Their motives for participation were equally varied. There was Gen. Juan Tomas Diaz, who was bitter because Trujillo had suddenly (and characteristically) retired him from the army in 1960. There was Gen. José Roman Fernandez, Secretary of the Armed Forces. Roman wanted money and power.

One of the most active and efficient of the conspirators was Antonio de la Maza. He wanted revenge. De la Maza thought that Trujillo had murdered his brother. There was young, good-natured Lt. Amado Garcia, formerly on Trujillo's personal staff. He wanted only to free his republic from tyranny. A score of other Dominicans participated directly or indirectly. All of the actual assassins—except Luis Amiama Tio and Antonio Imbert—are now dead.

The three Americans involved were less complex types. Mutt and Jeff—in subsequent confessions, the Dominican plotters referred to Jeff as a CIA agent—were merely doing their duty, obeying orders from Washington. With respect to the super market man, he didn't seem to have any official status. He just didn't like Trujillo, and never made any secret of that fact.

I can only speculate on the reasons why Washington wanted Trujillo killed. Was the order passed to shoot Trujillo because Trujillo had tried to bomb Betancourt? I don't think so. Cuba is probably the answer. Preparations for the Bay of Pigs operation were underway simultaneously with the development of the assassination plot which culminated a month after the Cuban fiasco.

I would wager that someone in the State Department had insisted that CIA's anti-Castro operation be balanced off by also knocking Trujillo out of the saddle. I would also wager that CIA was less than eager to take on the assignment. Not that the agency would have any scruples about

the job. But Dominican intelligence had worked closely with CIA, supplying information and analysis which the agency could never have come up with on its own. Moreover, Trujillo was personally acquainted with Colonel King, then chief of CIA's Latin American operations.

But CIA was as anxious to knock off Castro as the State Department was to torpedo Trujillo. So, both departments probably agreed, the left-wing dictatorship and the right-wing dictatorship would be destroyed simultaneously. It didn't work out quite that way, of course.

However, you've got to give the State Department credit: the Department can be better skilled than the CIA when it comes to cloak and daggering. A few weeks before Trujillo was to be assassinated, the State Department led the Old Man to believe that a restoration of relations might be possible. That was the gist of what Trujillo was told by Robert Murphy, former U.S. Under-Secretary of State.

As I understand it, society columnist Igor Cassini— whose public relations firm had been retained by Trujillo —told Joseph Kennedy, father of the U.S. President, that the Dominican Republic was about to explode in a Castro-type revolution. The elder Kennedy passed this very erroneous estimate on to his son. President Kennedy then contacted the State Department, which urged that Murphy be sent down. His mission was allegedly to explore possibilities of easing tensions between the two governments. This, at a time when the State Department was already far advanced on its *own* final solution of the Trujillo problem. Without his knowledge, Murphy was being used as a smokescreen.

But poor old Trujillo was delighted. He listened carefully when Murphy told him to scrub up his image, hold frequent press conferences, invite OAS observers to witness the coming elections, and generally liberalize his regime. Murphy said that the President and the State Department wouldn't dare call for restoration of relations until Trujillo improved his own relations with the press.

Trujillo said that he was resented by the press and State Department officials because he had been absolutely right about Fidel Castro's connections with Communism as early as 1949—and they had been wrong. He had given documented evidence about Castro's whole past to both a powerful American Senator, and the CIA. "They will never forgive me for that," he said. Trujillo warned that the U.S. would need every ally in Latin America that it could muster for the struggle with Castro.

Murphy then made an interesting prognostication:

"Well," he said, "pretty soon there won't be any Cuban problem. Castro is a dead duck."

The date was April 16, 1961.

This was a day before the Bay of Pigs. It was also about a *full year after* the U.S. Embassy first began working with the Dominican conspirators. As Gall says, the American's super market served as chief communications and liaison channel between the Consulate and the conspirators. A secondary line of contact was through a young, mild-mannered Dominican pediatrician, Dr. Roberto Reid Cabral. The spark plug of the Dominican group was not one of the high-ranking politicians and military men involved. It was Antonio de la Maza, an obscure businessman. The group met frequently at the home of General Diaz.

By early December, 1960, the conspiracy had shaped up to what was to be its final form. However, the big question for both the Consulate and the conspirators was still unanswered: Washington had not indicated its approval of the conspirators' plans for a post-Trujillo government. Messages flew back and forth from the American, Cabral, the Consulate and Washington. Jeff flew north to confer. On Christmas Day, 1960, the green light was flashed: General Roman could head a provisional government until 1962 when elections would be held. Tactical execution of the plot was the next step.

The five months of delay that followed were not the result of Trujillo's security measures. The Old Man's movements had become so habitual that they were almost ritualistic. He was equally accustomed to travelling without guards.

The real problem was the second phase of the conspiracy: the actual seizure of power after Trujillo was dead. Everything depended on seizing the controls of the Trujillo machine. The major obstacle to that objective was Ramfis, Gen. Rafael Trujillo, Jr. In the States, Ramfis was considered little more than a playboy, whose exploits with Kim Novak and Zsa Zsa Gabor had been wildly publicized. In the Dominican Republic, however, Ramfis was son and heir to Trujillo. Ramfis had sufficient influence to control the armed forces and block the coup. So he had to be removed from the scene.

Somebody came up with a proposal. Ramfis made periodic trips to Europe. If Trujillo were killed while Ramfis was in Europe, he could be expected to come racing back by air. But all regularly scheduled airline traffic between Europe and the Republic passed through the U.S. If the U.S. government cooperated, Ramfis could be stopped in New York. The U.S. government could then keep him forcibly under wraps until Roman consolidated his position.

The Consulate, and Washington, agreed. A stop order regarding the Trujillo family would be flashed to the Immigration Service immediately after the assassination. In addition, Roman was assured of U.S. military support, if needed. U.S. Marines would be available. Washington's involvement in the conspiracy was now total.

Plans for the coup were simple and logical. Trujillo would be ambushed on one of his weekly trips to his San Cristobal hacienda. His body would be hidden. Roman would announce that Trujillo had disappeared and simultaneously, as Secretary of the Armed Forces, he would proclaim a national emergency. Roman would automatically assume control of the machinery of state.

Ramfis, meanwhile, would be bottled up in the States. It was up to General Roman to handle all the other Trujillos. Quietly. If he needed help, Roman could call on the Marines—I have often wondered what ex-Marine Trujillo would have thought of that!—who would land on the pretext of "protecting American lives and property." The Marines would be followed by a task force of State Department officials who would help prop up the new regime. Finally, Roman in control, the new government would be formally recognized.

A nice plan, but almost every conceivable thing went wrong with it—except that Trujillo was indeed killed. One flaw was Roman himself. At the moment of truth, he wilted. Another was failure to provide for what we call the *imprevisto,* the unexpected. In this case—me. By pure coincidence, as I will explain later, I was the fly in the conspiratorial ointment.

The Washington officials involved also seem to have considered the scheme somewhat less than foolproof. In fact, at one point they panicked and tried to call the whole thing off. Gall has described that part of the confusion in his *New Republic* article:

"Plans for the intended assassination were worked out over the same period in which the abortive assault on Cuba was being prepared. However, when the CIA-organized April 17, 1961 invasion at the Bay of Pigs failed and world attention was focused on Washington's complicity in that operation, a postponement of the attempt on Trujillo's life was ordered because of the embarrassment another such failure might cause the United States. But the order to hold up came too late. According to what I was told in the Dominican Republic, the needed weapons were already in the hands of the conspirators, who refused appeals . . . to delay the assassination. They insisted on moving at the first opportunity. This came on May 30."

For Trujillo, that particular evening began the same as countless others. There was, however, one slight change of routine. Following his customary *paseo,* or walk, along George Washington Avenue, Trujillo beckoned to Roman and the two of them stepped into a limousine. They made a surprise inspection of the San Isidro air force base some ten miles from the city.

Both men soon returned and Trujillo resumed his usual schedule. He called for his 1957 Chevrolet and, unescorted, headed for San Cristobal. And death. I have often wondered how Roman felt when he was taking that last ride with the man he had betrayed and who was to die minutes later.

It was about 10:20 P.M. when the first shots were fired. Four of the conspirators had been parked and waiting since 8:00 P.M. Their mission was to follow Trujillo's Chevrolet when it passed. Two other cars were parked on ahead on opposite sides of the highway. They were to close in when the first car began firing.

Unwittingly, I was also to turn up at the scene. As was often the case, I had accompanied the Old Man on his *paseo* and had gone home when he had left with General Roman. I dismissed my driver for the night and sat down with a book. It was a torrid evening and my wife began to complain about the heat. She asked me to take her for a drive along the seashore boulevard.

We were pulling into a drive-in restaurant when Trujillo's car passed. I was just about to order cokes when I thought I heard bursts of machinegun fire in the distance. My first thought was that my ears were playing tricks on me. Then I suddenly remembered that Trujillo had passed in that direction a few moments before. That was enough. I swung back on the highway and raced toward the sound of shooting.

In less than a minute I came upon this scene:

Trujillo's Chevrolet was stopped in the center of the four-lane highway. On the right was a car facing in the same direction as the Chevrolet. On the left was another car with bright headlights which illuminated the scene. A third car was beyond and to the right, facing Trujillo's car. I could see men firing furiously at a figure who staggered into the beam of the headlights. The Old Man fired a last bullet, then pitched forward on his face. Trujillo was dead.

As in a trance, I drove slowly forward until I was almost on top of them. It was my wife's screams which brought me to my senses. I swung the car around and sped back to give the alarm.

I frantically began to collect my thoughts as I drove away. It was obvious that officers were involved; civilians could not have secured so many automatic weapons . . . I was also sure that the assassination was not an end in itself . . . it had to be coordinated with an invasion or coup, or both . . . we had been hearing reports that an invasion force was being organized in Venezuela.

I headed for the home of General Roman. As chief of the armed forces, he should be the first to know. I had not the slightest reason to doubt his loyalty. Trujillo had carefully filled the post of Secretary of the Armed Forces. Roman was related to the Trujillo family by marriage, had been given $200,000 by the Old Man, and was regarded as being a bit weak. I wondered if he was strong enough to cope with this.

Roman quivered visibly when I hurriedly reported what I had seen. "Have you told anybody else," he asked. "Are you sure he's dead?"

"Of course, I'm sure he's dead," I told him, "and I've come directly to you. You're in charge now. Come on, let's get busy."

Roman hesitated, his eyes on the floor. "Let's go," I repeated. Slowly, Roman followed me out the door.

He should have shot me. When he walked out of the house he doomed his coup and himself. I was the only one who knew Trujillo had been assassinated. He knew that I would take immediate action, upsetting their plans and timetable.

But Roman had no stomach for conspiracy. It was the measure of the man that he had insisted to the conspirators that he would take no action until he personally had seen Trujillo's corpse. He wanted to be damn well sure the Old Man was really dead before he started anything. The plan had been that Trujillo's corpse would be driven to Roman's house for his inspection. Instead, I turned up. Now Roman was not sure of anything, least of all himself. Docilely, he left with me.

The assassins telephoned the Roman house while we were gone. They were ready to show him the body. His wife told them that something terrible had happened and he had gone out with me. Demoralized, they went into hiding. Amiama made a final call. It was to the American Consulate.

At 5:00 a.m. that morning, Trujillo's body was found in the trunk of a car at the home of Juan Tomas Diaz—two blocks from the American Consulate.

Curiously, in view of the situation, the first official announcement of the killing came the following day from Kennedy's press agent, Pierre Salinger, in Paris. By that time, too, the Government knew the full ramifications of the conspiracy and the names of most of the assassins. They were hunted down and killed or captured. Only Imbert and Amiama survived.

In the U.S., the stop order on Trujillos netted only a

daughter, Flor de Oro, who vainly attempted to return in time to attend her father's funeral. Ramfis *chartered* an Air France liner, bypassing American territory.

Mutt exited the Dominican Republic with equal speed —and Jeff stayed put in Washington—despite the protective presence of a U.S. Navy task force just off shore. The State Department made it plain that it was ready to send in the Marines at the slightest pretext. Ramfis was "advised" to keep quiet and cooperate. Ramfis did both.

The facts behind the assassination had to be suppressed. Their exposure would have brought the wrath of Washington down on Ramfis and probably triggered anti-U.S. violence in the Dominican Republic—in which case the State Department would have its excuse to send Marines swarming ashore. I was given the word: the confessions of the captured assassins must be kept secret. The Dominican press was forbidden to speculate on the rumors beginning to sweep the country—even deleting from a wire service story a reference to U.S. involvement in the plot, made by Castro lieutenant Che Guevara. The Dominican government announced only that investigation indicated that "the assassination was backed by a political conspiracy involving a foreign government." Then the case was closed.

Assassination is a traditional feature of the claw and fang of Caribbean politics. None knew that better than Trujillo. I have never heard even the Old Man's friends condemn his murder on moral grounds. But I have heard both his friends and enemies denounce Mutt's and Jeff's absence from the country. By doing so, they abandoned their co-conspirators to their fates—and those fates were not pleasant.

As for Trujillo, I suspect that he would have been quite satisfied with his fate. A man who lived by the gun, he died triggering one, shooting it out with his enemies. But one thing puzzles me:

Trujillo, with his deep respect for machineguns, deliberately chose to fight it out, armed only with a pistol. He was not trapped there on the highway by any means. He was fired on from behind by automatic weapons, but ahead of him, as he well knew, was open highway to a military post a few minutes away. He had a fast car and an expert driver. He had a good chance of reaching safety. Instead, he stopped the car, got out and matched his pistol against machineguns.

Trujillo was committing suicide—and I think he knew it.

3

Empire

TRUJILLO'S reign ended as it had begun: in bloodshed and bursts of machinegun fire. That sort of thing has been traditional in Dominican politics. It is a claw and fang struggle for survival. Trujillo was able to survive for 31 years only because he was almost perfectly adapted to, and shaped by, that environment. I think that too much attention has been focussed on the person of Trujillo, too little on what produced him. So let's take a brief look at the history of my country.

For centuries, Dominicans have referred to their country as "The land Columbus loved best." But Dominicans also had reason to fear that theirs was the land that God must love least. Our whole history is one of foreign invasions and domestic insurrections. From our first independence from Spain, in 1821, to 1916, when the United States occupied the Dominican Republic, our country suffered more than a hundred violent political upheavals. A seemingly endless series of foreign and revolutionary armies ravaged the countryside. Communications between the capital, Santo Domingo City, and the provinces was almost nil.

From this chaos there emerged regional chiefs, known as *caciques*. These were very tough individuals who had clawed their way to local leadership and held it until someone a bit tougher came along. The central government was almost powerless to control the caciques. Dominican politics consisted of several caciques periodically getting together to overthrow the government.

The Dominican government was never strong enough to resist the caciques. The army was merely a handful of ill-trained conscripts. Recruitment was simple. From time to time the government would call on loyal caciques for volunteers. The local chiefs would then round up a batch of unhappy youths and send them to the capital. Sometimes it was necessary to use force. One cacique handcuffed his "volunteers" to a huge rope and sent them to the army with this message: "Here are your volunteers. Please return the rope."

But the U.S. Marines and Trujillo changed all that. In 1916 the Marines landed and occupied the Dominican Republic. They confiscated and dumped into the sea some 3,000,000 small arms—enough to supply three weapons to every man, woman and child in the country—built roads and trained a constabulary. The Marines groomed Lt. Rafael Trujillo and other tough, competent officers to command the new Dominican army.

It may be considered a left-handed compliment to the Corps, but Trujillo always thought of himself as basically a Marine Corps officer—and "damned proud of it." It was typical, for instance, that of the 40 to 50 decorations conferred upon him during his long career, Trujillo was proudest of a faded, threadbare medal attesting to his service with the Marines.

This loyalty to the Corps was responsible for his unwavering loyalty to the United States. This was true even in the face of Washington's rebuffs and attempts to topple him. Trujillo never got over his love affair with the Marines.

The Marines pulled out in 1924. Behind them they left that small but efficient army and a network of roads. The roads penetrated to the formerly isolated regions ruled by the caciques. And the new Marine-trained army had become more than a match for the caciques' *pistoleros.*

By 1930, Trujillo had become chief of staff. In the best traditions of Dominican politics, he ousted the president and took over. That was easy. But how to stay in power? Trujillo knew he wouldn't last a year if the caciques weren't finally brought to heel.

So Trujillo crushed the caciques. Moving his Marine-trained troops over Marine-built roads, the Generalissimo struck again and again. Caciques who wouldn't surrender unconditionally were gunned down. The survivors saw the light. The era of regional warlords was ended. The Era of Trujillo had begun.

For his own reasons, Trujillo then precipitated a social revolution. He was not of the aristocracy. He feared and resented the old families, a feeling that most of them heartily reciprocated. So Trujillo addressed himself directly to the *compesinos*, the peasants. The power of the caciques is broken, he told them, and you are now under the protection of my government. Thousands of letters were sent out urging the peasants to submit their complaints directly to Trujillo. Were they abused by the landowners? Tell Trujillo. Did a village need a schoolhouse? Ask Trujillo. Perhaps it could be arranged.

The campesinos never did realize that they had only changed masters. Trujillo was a cynical realist. He knew that the army officers and aristocrats were potentially dangerous. Sooner or later, they would combine to oust him. So Trujillo set out to mesmerize the masses who provide the manpower for those officers and aristocrats.

One of the techniques he used was baptism—baptism and hundred dollar bills. Trujillo became godfather to tens of thousands of children. And the parents of each child received a hundred dollars. Trujillo also reaped a dividend: it is considered poor form in Latin America to conspire against your *compadre*, the godfather of your child.

These baptisms had to be seen to be believed. Shabbily dressed women of the lower classes, holding squalling infants, woud stream through the heavily guarded gate of the National Palace and line up outside the Palace chapel.

The Old Man would handle the proceedings on a production-line basis. He would beam briefly at each mother and child, mumble a few words, then pass on to the next. The din was terrific and the atmosphere inside the chapel was stifling. But it went on for hours, day after day. Let no one say that Trujillo didn't work hard at being dictator.

And it worked. The masses remained loyal to Trujillo to the end. When he was buried, tens of thousands of grief-stricken campesinos poured out of the hills to attend his funeral. Yes, like it or not, the man was popular with the masses. No member of the educated classes ever dared attempt to lead a popular revolution. No colonel ever dared order his troops to march on the National Palace. His own men would have mowed him down. That is why the men who finally assassinated Trujillo were all from the upper ranks of Dominican society, and even they dared to act only in concert with agents of the U.S. government.

Trujillo's political tactics also produced another social transformation: the appearance of a middle class. In 1930 there were only three really wealthy families in the Dominican Republic—the Vicinis, Ricarts and Espaillats—plus another fifty landed families of moderate wealth. Below them were only the masses. There was nothing in between.

There were several reasons for the absence of a middle class. One was that the ever-recurring revolutions ruined agriculture, the country's only major source of income. Harvests rotted while field hands shot at each other in opposing armies. Not enough wealth could be generated to produce any real business or businessmen.

What few merchants there were made it a point to live from hand to mouth. They kept very little merchandise in stock. And they had good reason, for anything of value in the stores was invariably confiscated by one or another of the rebel armies which made their annual appearance.

Trujillo's iron-fisted dictatorship changed all that. He

shot people who distrubed the peace. And with peace, the republic's natural wealth burst forth. Agricultural production soared. A commercial and professional class came into being. The population of the Dominican Republic nearly tripled in the Era of Trujillo.

The price was freedom. Trujillo imposed a military discipline which turned the population into an army. The Dominican government was commanded with the same military efficiency that Trujillo had so admired in the Marines. For the first time, and possibly the last, public employees went to work on time. Official functions were conducted on a precise schedule. Offenses were punished in the same spirit of a commanding officer meting out disciplinary action. And anti-Trujillo activity, to the Old Man, was the same as a soldier committing mutiny.

Trujillo systematically reduced the country's top officers and officials to a state of complete docility. One of the more subtle techniques was the routine called "el paseo," his evening stroll. It seems that years ago a doctor had told Trujillo that people who walked a lot didn't suffer from heart trouble. Trujillo took the advice to heart.

Everyday, whatever the weather, he took his walk. It became a sacred institution. Moreover, Trujillo didn't like to walk alone. So every evening all high-ranking officers had to wait for him *outside* his home to accompany the Old Man on his stroll. There was no set time, so the brass often had to wait an hour or more before Trujillo would decide to come out. And Trujillo, a human dynamo, used his tremendous physical energy to awe his officers. He set a pace which exhausted men decades his junior.

Once Trujillo remained at an official ball until 3:00 A.M. That meant that the top officers with him also had to stay— none could leave before he did. The next morning he was at his desk at the usual 8:00 A.M., firing off phone calls which blasted scores of hungover officers and officials out of their beds.

Less subtle disciplinary tactics were used with the Dominican man in the street. The following incident was typical.

The Generalissimo ordered that the national anthem be played each time the Dominican flag was raised or lowered over the National Palace. The Palace at that time overlooked Columbus Square in the heart of the capital. It didn't take long for Trujillo to notice that the loungers in the popular square didn't pay any attention to the flag ceremony.

One morning, soldiers clad in civilian clothes swarmed into the square. They clobbered everyone who didn't stand up for the anthem and flag. This went on for several days. Then people began drifting out of the square just before each ceremony. Trujillo responded by throwing a cordon of troops around the area. People eventually got the message. Dominicans were soon leaping frantically to their feet at the sound of the first notes of the anthem.

Such tactics led to many a whispered joke. Typical was the one about the Dominican dog who trotted across the border into the impoverished neighboring country of Haiti. A gaunt Haitian dog stared at the sleek visitor. "You must be mad," he told the Dominican canine. "Why did you come to this land of hunger?" "Why did I come here?" replied the other dog, "why I came to bark, to bark!"

Nevertheless, few Dominicans seriously opposed Trujillo and his methods—most being content to bear with a system that admittedly offered some rewards for the loss of freedom. Some, however, did. One was a prominent citizen, respected as one of the best brains in the republic. Trujillo wanted him on his team. But the man refused one government post after another. Finally, Trujillo sent an aide to see the man. "Perhaps it is the Generalissimo's job that you want?" the aide asked pointedly. The threat didn't have to be spelled out. Trujillo quickly had himself a new Cabinet Minister.

Between these two extremes were those who approved of the progress and stability Trujillo had brought to the Dominican Republic, but who did not condone Trujillo's methods. This type of man would wrestle with his conscience, and then, eventually, serve Trujillo—blinding himself to the sordid side of the regime. Some assured themselves that they would exercise a moderating influence on the dictator. Such men did some good, if not a great deal. Trujillo was not particularly interested in being led onto the paths of righteousness.

In any event, Trujillo attracted to him the best brains and most powerful men in the country. In one way or another, they were pressed into service. There were, of course, a few exceptions. But one estimate is that no more than six prominent Dominicans denied their support to Trujillo. This, I think, is one of the most interesting accomplishments of the Era of Trujillo.

Most of those men turned against Trujillo at the end, of course. Some had had their sons killed or tortured for anti-Trujillo activities. Others had been abused by Trujillo beyond endurance. But most simply deserted a sinking ship. Latins sense a weakening leadership. They are realists in such matters. A faltering leader is abandoned and his former supporters turn on him, eager to be in on the kill. So it is with the animals of the jungle, and Latin politics are best described by this analogy.

Trujillo was constantly aware of the quicksilverish nature of his support. He soaked up the torrent of flattery, made sure that the praise was made a matter of public record, but never really trusted anyone.

The Dominican Republic had a Congress of sorts under Trujillo, a Congress which he carefully stocked with the loudest and most docile *trujillistas*. This was still not enough for the Old Man. Each deputy and senator had to turn in a signed letter of resignation, the date left blank, when he took office. Eventually, even the pre-signing of a letter of resignation was discarded as a formality. Many a Congressman would be sitting down to breakfast in the morning when he would get a call informing him that there was no need for him to leave for work, inasmuch as he had just resigned. The alleged resignation would be read in session and that was that. Never did a Congressman protest. The turnover of Congressmen was tremendous.

As for the judiciary, its function may best be described by the following incident:

A visiting American once asked a Dominican lawyer what the penalty was for accidental shooting while hunting.

The lawyer reflected a moment. "Well," he said; "that would depend on who shot whom."

Cabinet Ministers were little more than office boys, for Trujillo was at the vital center of everything. He was his own Secretary of the Armed Forces, Foreign Relations, Finance, Interior, etc.

I recall a typical incident in a cabinet meeting when Joaquin Balaguer was figurehead-president:

The Secretary of Education read a report stating that there would be no classroom space in the coming year for some 30,000 children in the Federal District. Trujillo, who insisted on going through the formalities, raised his hand.

"Mr. President, may I speak?"

"Oh, yes, Sir," said the President.

"Mr. President, I ask you to appoint me Secretary of Education."

"Oh, yes, Sir," said the President.

"It would be the salvation of Dominican education," quavered the Secretary of Education.

"Mr. President," said Trujillo, "If I were Secretary of Education, there would be no nonsense about inadequate classroom space."

"That is true, Sir," said the President.

"That is very, *very* true, Sir," repeated the Secretary.

"However, I am here merely in an unofficial capacity. I trust you will resolve this problem. Double them up if necessary. I don't care how you do it. If you can't, I will. Well?"

"We will, Sir," chorused the President and Secretary.

"Very well, I withdraw my application for the post."

There was always a weird air of unreality to the Dominican Government. That was because there were really two Governments: One that was official and phony, the other that was unofficial and very real. Huge government buildings were erected to house bureaus and officials which served no real purpose. Mechanically, the machinery of the façade government moved, but only as meaningless play-acting. Trujillo was the Government and the Government was Trujillo.

4

"Corporation President"

HOW could Trujillo cope with the titanic task of being literally a one-man government? Mostly through incessant hard work. His working day began at 5 every morning of his life. He followed a schedule so rigid, incidentally, that it was to make easy his assassination.

As soon as he was awake, Trujillo reached for the intelligence reports prepared during the night. Then he read the latest UPI and AP releases which had come in over his personal teletype machines. He was in his office in the lower left wing corner of the National Palace by 8 A.M. Lunch at the Palace began promptly at 11:30 A.M. Then a short walk and back to his residence.

He returned to the Palace at 3 P.M., worked until about six, and then visited his mother. Later in the evening he took his other walk, the famous *paseo.* Frequently the Old Man would then ride around the city in a small car and without escort—"to get the feel of the town." He was usually in bed by ten. Often, however, Trujillo would stay up until the dawn hours. But he would still rise at five.

If this schedule does not seem overly strenuous, I should make it absolutely clear that the Old Man never stopped working at top efficiency during his waking hours—with the sole exception of the times he would relax with one of his girl friends. On Sunday afternoons, Trujillo would leave the Palace at noon and go to the late races. Invariably, however, just as much business would be transacted in his box as at the office.

It was also part of strict routine that in the middle of the week he would leave for his huge cattle ranch at nearby San Cristobal. Harried Palace officials would sigh with relief, but for Trujillo it was business as usual. His day would begin at 5 A.M. with the intelligence reports rushed to him by messenger. Important conferences would be held at the ranch and he was in constant telephone contact with the capital, other parts of the Dominican Republic, and even the United States.

The ranch did permit two distractions. Free from the burden of maintaining his image, Trujillo would relax and ponder developments. After a quiet hour or two, the Old Man would then send for his current mistress. . . .

Back at his Palace desk a day or two later, Trujillo would be confronted by enormous stacks of routine reports, files, memorandums. Each communication had been summarized to its bare essence by a staff of efficient secretaries. Still, the sheer volume of the documents was almost overwhelming. But Trujillo ploughed through them like a threshing machine. If the summary interested him, he would glance at the original. If the case warranted, he would study the document with care, but always with prodigious speed. Usually, matters relating to the armed forces, finances and intelligence were given a thorough treatment. A line across the paper meant thumbs down. His initials plus one or two words scrawled on the document meant that action was to be taken.

A fantastic memory and his Marine Corps-instilled sense of administrative organization made possible Trujillo's ability to sweep his desk clear of paperwork. He was also mentally versatile, being able to shift instantly from intelligence to public works to foreign affairs. But once his mind was fixed on a subject, he gave it absolute concentration. He would not leave it until he had reached a decision. There was no "pending" basket on his desk.

His memory was incredible. Any report on any subject was never forgotten. If he read a report at variance with anything he had read before, a bell rang in his mind. He would spot the discrepancy instantly and call for the previous report. His secretaries would be told what it was about, who sent it, and when.

This memory, coupled with his powerful personality, was also a devastating weapon in reducing the army to docility. Officers too lax or too ambitious would receive Trujillo's personal treatment, which usually went like this:

The officer would be summoned into Trujillo's presence. He would enter the office, salute and come to attention before Trujillo's desk. Trujillo, who would be reading, would ignore the man. After a minute or two, the Old Man would look up as if noticing the officer for the first time. Then, gazing fixedly into the man's eyes, Trujillo would start firing questions.

Heaven help the officer who didn't have the right answers! Trujillo—I will say this for him—always did. I saw strong men leave his office pale and shaking after these sessions. He was able to project an almost physical force when he wished, and he knew it. Once, under fire myself, I caught myself thinking, "My God, he's looking right into my mind. He knows what I'm thinking!"

This was the man of whom Miami *Herald* columnist Jack Kofoed once wrote:

"His face was expressionless. It seldom gave an indication of his feeling. You could call it deadpan except for his eyes. They were the strangest I've ever seen, soft almost like a woman's—not the eyes of a man said to have ordered the murder of hundreds while clawing his way to the top and staying there."

Kofoed was right on one point: Trujillo's face was usually an expressionless mask. As for those eyes, they were soft when Kofoed saw them because that was the image Trujillo was projecting. When he was angry or when he wanted to give that impression those eyes became like frozen bullets.

I have read much nonsense about Trujillo's losing his temper, personally torturing prisoners, and booting the President in the rear from time to time. All that was written by people who didn't know Trujillo. Never once did I see him get excited or raise his voice. He was too aloof for real anger. And his time and energy were too precious to waste by berating mere mortals. Unruffled and unperturbed, Trujillo operated like a powerful machine.

Not that Trujillo didn't have foibles like everybody else. In many ways, he was altogether too human. He liked women, and they liked him. He didn't like planes and television. He didn't think air conditioning was healthy—being a health nut, he kept in training like a professional athlete —and his tiny, stuffy office was usually stifling. But Trujillo never sweated; his visitors usually did, profusely, putting them at a great psychological disadvantage.

There was one flaw in his emotional armor: Trujillo was dangerously moody. On an emotional upswing, the Old Man was apt to fling money around like a mad Santa Claus. There are people in the States today who are rich because they approached the Old Man with crazy propositions on one of his good days. And there are people in the Dominican Republic who are deep in their graves because they crossed Trujillo when he was feeling depressed.

Trujillo, who had a natural flair and cultivated an air of mystery, adored drama. He was a ham and he appreciated that quality in others. If you went to him and said, "Chief, my wife has cancer, my nine children are suffering from scrofula, and I've lost my job," he might have given you fifty pesos. If you went in and waved your arms, wept and

fell in a heap at his feet, he would probably have granted
your wish for a binge at Miami Beach—and given you
$5,000 spending money. He was that way.

Trujillo's affinity for theatrics and fantasy began to
assume ludicrous proportions the year before he was killed.
The Old Man decided to stage a spectacular show to prove
that he wasn't what he was. The theme was that Trujillo
was no dictator; Trujillo had retired. So had all the other
Trujillos. Brother Hector Trujillo was fired as titular president. It was announced that elections would be held. The
Generalissimo, carried away with his performance, even
went so far as to have himself referred to as "Citizen
Trujillo."

Some one—I think it was New York lawyer Morris Ernst
—suggested to the Old Man that he emulate Kemal
Ataturk, the national hero of Turkey. It seems that Ataturk,
to avoid being labeled a dictator, resigned from his own
party to set up a party in opposition to the government. At
this point, the Old Man was willing to try anything. He
resigned from his Dominican Party and announced that
he was joining one of the three or four phony political
parties which he ordered into existence.

The Old Man announced that he was going to run for the
governorship of Santiago province. The "election" was
never held. At another time, Trujillo appointed himself
Governor of the Central Bank. On still another occasion,
Citizen Trujillo decided that being Dominican ambassador
to the United Nations might be an effective front. He made
a real production of it. Visualize this scene:

It was a bright Caribbean morning. The presidential
guard, 150 men, resplendent in blue and gold dress uniforms, was drawn up in formation in front of the National
Palace. The press and government officials crowded the
palace steps. This was the day that Citizen Trujillo was to
pay his respects to the President and receive final instructions before departing for the U.N.

Precisely at 10 A.M., Trujillo's huge black limousine

swung through the Palace gates, up the winding driveway, and came to a halt in front of the Palace steps. Sabers and bayonets flashed as the guard presented arms. A bugle sounded and the presidential band crashed forth with ruffles and flourishes. From the Ozama Fortress, a mile away, artillery boomed a 21-gun salute.

Trujillo emerged from the limousine. He stood there, ramrod-stiff, face expressionless, as the band played the national anthem. The music ended and there was a burst of spontaneous applause from the onlookers.

Yes, it was spontaneous. None knew better than the men gathered there, his lieutenants and hirelings, of the evil side of their *jefe*. This was a man who was totally ruthless, amoral, who had killed again and again, who would kill more before he finally fell. But there was also an animal magnificence about Trujillo. Erect, defiant, almost contemptuously he faced his enemies. Whatever else he was, Trujillo was one hell of a man.

He was also one hell of a charlatan.

Trujillo strode up the Palace steps and down the hall to Balaguer's office. The onlookers crowded in to listen to a meaningless ceremonial dialogue between "Mr. President" and "Citizen Trujillo." The new "U.N. Delegate" and his entourage then swept back down the hall to the Palace steps.

Again the band blared, the guns boomed, troops presented arms. Trujillo stepped back in the car and sped off through the Palace gates. Officially, Dictator Trujillo was no more.

Fifteen minutes later another car entered the Palace grounds by the rear entrance. Trujillo got out and went back to work.

The "U.N. appointment"? Nobody even bothered to wonder. The "corporation president" was back at his desk busy with sugar, internal security, Caribbean affairs, and, perhaps, a secret meeting with one of the many American officials on his payroll. . . .

5

Bullets and Birdseed

TRUJILLO survived for 31 years because he elevated the law of the jungle into a science. Instinctively, he understood the principles of political combat. He hated Communism, for instance, with savage passion. Yet, Trujillo and the Reds had much in common. Mao Tse-tung's maxim, "Power blooms out of the mouth of a gun," summed up Trujillo's own thinking exactly. He believed in guns. And in himself.

Once, in a reminiscent mood, Trujillo told me of an incident which took place when he first took power.

"It was back in 1930, when I had just ousted the President, that I received a message from an old friend, a Marine Corps Colonel, stationed in Haiti. The Colonel asked me to meet him on the border for an important conference.

"When I arrived, my friend told me that he was acting as spokesman for the State Department. The Colonel had been instructed to tell me that the State Department did not approve of me. They wanted a civilian to be President.

"I told the Colonel that, nevertheless, I would not withdraw from the elections. My friend was silent for a moment.

"Then he pointed at the sub-machineguns carried by my escort. 'Trujillo, do you have many of those?' 'Yes,' I answered, 'I have enough.' 'Good,' he said. 'Don't tell them I said so, but go ahead. You'll be all right.'

"A very practical man, my friend the Colonel," Trujillo nodded approvingly.

It was in 1960 that he told me the anecdote. Those guns

had kept him in power 30 years. But the following year he was to be cut down by another group of men who also had plenty of machineguns. Trujillo had come full cycle.

Despite Trujillo's great respect for military power, he distrusted all military men. The Dominican Army, far from being a Praetorian Guard, was kept in a state of frightened subjugation. Trujillo took every precaution to guard himself against a military coup. Officers were shifted constantly from post to post, and were ruthlessly purged at the slightest provocation.

Trujillo never missed an opportunity to hammer home the fact that he was boss. The following incident was typical:

The Old Man promoted a brash young Navy Commander to two-star Admiral and made him Chief of the Navy. The Officer was overwhelmed by his sudden importance. He came to believe that he had acquired his stars by merit, not by Trujillo's whim. Our new Admiral began to fancy himself a sort of Dominican Lord Nelson. That interested Trujillo.

Matters came to a head at a luncheon in the National Palace. I was present as Under-Secretary of the Armed Forces. In the course of the meal, Trujillo turned to the Admiral and asked him why he thought he had been given his post.

The "right" answer was "Because you were kind enough to appoint me, my Chief." But our boy was out of touch with reality. He plunged into a long discourse on the improvements he was making in the Navy. By the time the Admiral had finished talking, he was back to Commander.

The Navy man had forgotten Standard Operating Procedure—and SOP dominated Trujillo and Trujillo dominated the country. Once Trujillo gave an order or set a pattern it became SOP. The whole structure of the Dominican State was composed of SOP's. The Dominican Republic was not merely a police state. It was a military post.

Trujillo's SOP's were designed to achieve military efficiency as well as keep the military under control. But, inevitably, they worked too well. For instance, long after Marine Corps wide brim hats and leggings had become obsolete, they were still in use by the Dominican Army. That made procurement difficult and prompted me to send a memorandum to the Chief of Staff proposing a change.

The Chief of Staff, horrified, sent for me immediately. He showed me an Army general order signed by Trujillo years ago. The order prescribed the hats and leggings. It was no use arguing. The General wasn't about to change the SOP or even propose a change.

Another example of Trujillo's personnel management was his use of human lightning rods. By that I mean Trujillo always had some henchman who drew public criticism which should have been directed against Trujillo himself. For years, a top aide named Anselmo Paulino performed that role. Paulino had a glass eye. Dominicans, with their penchant for nicknames, referred to him as "The Magic Eye."

Paulino was supposed to wield great power and be very evil, neither of which was true. Paulino was merely a tool, diverting popular hatred from Trujillo to himself. Paulino lost his position—and almost his life—when he stopped thinking of himself as a tool and began to regard himself as a necessity. Trujillo, a self-contained unit, needed no one.

Trujillo's top aides had to be very careful even in expressing opinions, unless he asked for suggestions. The members of the Old Man's staff were not even supposed to discuss their work with each other. Each aide was told only what he had to know and no more. This was true not only in intelligence, but in all other fields. No one was to know all that was going on. Only Trujillo held all the strings.

As another safety device, Trujillo delighted in playing one aide or officer against another. He was constantly stirring the pot, arousing envy, ambition, resentment. The reason? To guarantee that the most powerful government officials and army officers would never trust each other. They could never unite in common front. They could only vie for Trujillo's favor.

And all this was capped off by his famous practice of naming relatives to top political and military posts.

I was one of the few top officers who was not related to Trujillo. And I didn't last long in a command position. I was placed on the reserve list as a Major General at the ripe old age of 37.

Never in all the many years I was close to Trujillo did I see him exhibit real friendship toward a man in uniform. In my own case, our relationship became much more relaxed and friendly after I was placed on the reserve list and changed to civilian clothes. Only then did the Old Man feel free to consult with me on top military, political and intelligence matters.

This policy was summed up by a phrase Trujillo liked to quote: "The best way to prevent fires is to allow no one to get hold of a box of matches." To Trujillo, power and knowledge were dangerously inflammable.

Up until 1957, however, repression in the Dominican Republic had been efficient, but haphazard. In that year, facing now the active opposition of the United States, Trujillo decided to pull all the loose ends together by creating a Department of Security. The new department was to coordinate all matters relating to intelligence, counterintelligence, law enforcement and immigration. The Security Department included the National Police, the Military Intelligence Service (SIM), Foreign Intelligence, and Immigration.

Since I had long worked in Foreign Intelligence and because Trujillo wanted an Army general to head up the Department, I became the first Secretary of Security. I didn't fancy myself as a junior Himmler, however, and my term of office lasted exactly four months and ten days.

Believe it or not, Trujillo was so disgusted by my negative attitude toward my job that he sent me to an army hospital psychiatric ward to check my sanity. This dangerous farce ended when Trujillo's brother, Hector, put in a good word for me.

So I was transferred to a new post. I, a West Pointer, was made of all things, Inspector General of the Navy. My successor, Major General Felix Hermida, was an equally reluctant dragon. Once again, Hector came to the rescue and Hermida was retired. That was the end of the Department of Security. But it was replaced by something infinitely worse.

Trujillo had never really trusted the Army. Now, two career generals had failed him. And it was just then that Johnny Abbes, a civilian, accurately called the shots on the assassination of Guatemalan President Carlos Castillo Armas—which was precisely the kind of conspiracy Trujillo himself feared most. So the Old Man decided to build a powerful new SIM, a SIM civilian-led and largely civilian-staffed.

The Chief had found his man. Abbes, intelligent, energetic and ruthless, built the SIM into an apparatus feared and hated by both civilians and military. For the first time, the Dominican Republic suffered organized brutality on a massive scale. The infamous "Cuarenta," a house of torture, flourished.

At this point, let's take a closer look at Trujillo the man. What made him tick? On the one hand he was capable of literally hauling Santo Domingo into the twentieth century. On the other hand, he was equally capable of perpetrating monstrous crimes against the people who dwelt in his "New Homeland."

First of all, consider Trujillo's innate characteristics. From the beginning he was ruthless, intelligent, efficient. He was a master politician of the pure Machiavellian breed. But Trujillo, who began as an army officer and evolved into politician, eventually became a near-deity, a demigod.

There is a broad element of fakery and charlatanism in the makeup of most Latin leaders. There has to be. Flamboyance is expected of Latin politicians. For their part, the people respond overwhelmingly to successful politicians and to power itself. Support for the leader becomes passionate adulation. Eventually, the leader begins to take the adulation seriously.

That happened in the Dominican Republic. Long before Madison Avenue invented the term, Trujillo was creating his "image." He founded a political party for the purpose of ramming that image into every corner of the Republic. For thirty years not a single day passed that the Dominican people were not exposed to praises of the glory of Trujillo. It was, as Madison Avenue might express it, a saturation campaign.

If the Government built a bridge, Trujillo had built the bridge. If the Government balanced the budget, Trujillo had balanced the budget. No one had ever built anything in the republic or balanced the budget before, so all the hocus pocus was very effective.

Hospitals, schools and other public works, cities and provinces were named after Trujillo and his family. Innumerable statues, monuments and busts were erected in his honor. Officially, Trujillo's titles were *el Benefactor* and *Padre de la Patria Nueva*. Unofficially he was addressed as "Illustrious Chief," "Trujillo the Great," "Exalted Leader," and so on. No form of address could do justice to the magnificence of the Great One.

Endlessly, Trujillo extracted praise, pledges of loyalty committments and so forth from Dominicans of all classes. There was shrewd political reasoning behind that seeming egomania, for a man publicly stamped as an ardent *tru-*

jillista was thereby made to feel that he had placed his neck on the same block with that of the Old Man, and that his fortunes were linked with that of the regime.

It was only partially successful, of course. The men who assassinated Trujillo were public *trujillistas*. The governing National Council, which took over when the last of the Trujillos were ousted, was composed of men who had long and loudly sung the praises of the dictator.

I think it is of more than academic importance to probe into the "why" of that situation. Why did Dominicans lend their support to what was probably the most absolute dictatorship in the history of this hemisphere? I don't think Dominicans are essentially different from any other people. I think the answer could be applied to almost any dictatorship, or even strong government.

One reason is simple enough. It is summed up in the answer given Trujillo when he asked a prominent American intellectual to make a speech on his behalf.

"I would be delighted," the man told Trujillo, "but if you want the birds to sing you have to feed them birdseed." Trujillo got the point. He sent the man $10,000. The bird sang. For years, Trujillo scattered millions of dollars in birdseed all over the hemisphere and the birds chirruped happily.

6

Aphrodisia, Mafia
and Kickback

To Trujillo, money was like machineguns: a tool of
power. But if scattering that birdseed was expensive, so
were machineguns. As a result, the Old Man worked as
feverishly at making money as he did spending it. He built
a vast semi-official business organization coordinated by
what was called the *Oficina Particular del Generalisimo*,
the Generalissimo's Private Office. This "private" business
office was located in the National Palace.

This office got itself involved in some mighty odd business ventures. Promoters and business sharpies were
irresistibly drawn to Trujillo. For his part, perhaps because
he considered them kindred spirits, the Generalissimo often
couldn't resist taking a flyer in various oddball enterprises.
Like the following:

"PEGA PALO—The Vine that Makes you Virile. It grows
deep in the jungles of the Dominican Republic, and medical
authorities attest that this amazing plant restores youthful
vigor to men who have long since resigned as Romeos. . . ."

That was the title and lead to an article which appeared
in *Confidential* magazine in November, 1956. It was also
the beginning of one of the most curious episodes in the
Era of Trujillo. The Generalissimo went into the aphro-

disiac business. The American State Department took a dim view of the situation generally and Pega Palo specifically. This was made clear in a report sent to Washington by the U.S. Embassy in Ciudad Trujillo:

AIR POUCH

AM EMBASSY-CIUDAD TRUJILLO, D.R.

January 25th 1957

CERP-D, 22

INTRODUCTION OF PATENT MEDICINE KNOWN AS "PEGA PALO" IN THE UNITED STATES

Summary

Since the publication of an article in *Confidential* magazine on "Pega Palo," a vine that grows wild in the Dominican Republic and considered by some as an aphrodisiac, the Embassy has received numerous letters from individuals in the United States who are interested in obtaining "Pega Palo." Letters with similar requests have been received by the National Palace, the local Chamber of Commerce, hotels, the Department of Industry and Commerce and over 1,800 by the *Laboratorio Quimico Dominicano, C. por A.*, the holder of the Dominican trademark on this name. On December 17, 1956, this Laboratory signed a contract with Mr. W. L. Bridges, President of Bridges Company, P.O. Box 8353, South Moore Station, Houston Texas, giving the latter exclusive right for the importation and distribution of "Pega Palo" ("Fortidom" as it is now known) in the United States. It is understood that the Bridges Company has registered the name "Pega Palo" in all 48 States of the United States. Bridges appears to be backed by a group of fairly well-to-do Texas businessmen. . . .

In the weeks that followed the first excitement over "Pega Palo" Dr. Soba received visits from a number of Americans interested in marketing this product. He negotiated with two groups of Texans who offered sub-

stantial sums of money for the marketing rights of the
product in the United States, finally settling on the
Bridges Company. Bridges is understood to have paid
$25,000 in cash for the United States marketing rights . . .
for five years. . . .

It is the Embassy's opinion that "Pega Palo" or its
pharmaceutical name, "Fortidom," is a patent medicine
without any true aphrodisiac qualities. This is based on
a series of inquiries conducted by the Embassy in recent
weeks. It is reliably stated that "Pega Palo" is merely a
popular phrase meaning "have a shot," among other
possible meanings, as well as the popular name for a vine
growing in the mountains along the Haitian border
known as "Rauwolphia Pyramidadis," in scientific terms.
A series of experiments conducted by Dr. Soba did have
a mild tonic effect on otherwise healthy people. No indication was found that it had any sexually stimulating
qualities. These latter were invented "out of whole cloth"
by the writer of the *Confidential* article, possibly aided
by popular superstitions that the vine had aphrodisiac
characteristics.

Following the sales success of the patent medicine
"Hadacol" in the Southern States in recent years, many
Americans appear to be hopeful that large profits can
be realized from the sale of "Pega Palo." From the
Dominican side, both the Dominican Government and
the Dominican Chemical Laboratory are expecting to
realize substantial sums of money from the promotion
and sale of this product. The numerous letter writers and
callers who have approached the Embassy for help in
securing a supply of "Pega Palo" have been uniformly
advised that no scientific proof exists of the herb's efficiency as an aphrodisiac. It is probable, however, that
claims along this line will be made by the individuals,
both Dominican and American, who are promoting the
sale of this product. Such claims should be carefully

scrutinized by the Food and Drug Administration and the Federal Trade Commission.

> For the Ambassador
> (signed) Richard H. Stephens
> Second Secretary of Embassy

What Mr. Stephens apparently didn't know was that the story had been carefully planted in *Confidential*—by Trujillo himself. Overnight, we in the Dominican Government found ourselves peddling sex.

And what a business it was! Letters poured in by the thousands, letters filled with pleas and accompanied by currency or money orders. Some were addressed to Trujillo, others, in desperation, were marked "Any Citizen, Dominican Republic," and still others swamped the American Embassy. Pega Palo cocktails appeared in the tourist bars and Pega Palo *merengues* were introduced. Tourists and businessmen swarmed in, eager to buy the stuff by the ton or at least to gulp down the foul-tasting concoction. It all was quite a lesson in human behavior.

Things went beautifully for a while. But then some spoilsport in Washington decided that Pega Palo ran afoul of the Pure Food and Drug Act. It couldn't be exported to the U.S.—couldn't officially, but was anyway. Somehow, Pega Palo continued to find its way north.

Then one day in March, 1957, a short, fat individual came to my office. He introduced himself (let's call him "Eli X" of the Blank Steel Corporation of Chicago) and said he wanted to talk about Pega Palo. I was willing to listen.

"First of all, let us understand each other," he said, perspiring and wiping his misty spectacles. "Pega Palo is commercial and Pega Palo is sex. That means, if you market it in the States you do it through us. I represent the Syndicate."

"What syndicate?"

"*The* Syndicate," he answered irritably, "the mob, the

Mafia, the Combine or whatever you want to call it. What's the matter, don't you read the papers down here?"

Here we go again, I groaned mentally. Ever since the *Confidential* story, nuts from all over the United States had been rolling in. Now we had a guy who thought he was Murder, Inc.

"That's very interesting," I told him.

"Look," Eli said leaning forward, "I know what you're thinking." He fished in his pocket and pulled out several calling cards. "Have your Chicago consulate get in touch with the Blank Steel Corporation and they'll put you in contact with people who can vouch for me. You check me out and I'll contact you in a couple of days."

Intrigued, I did check up—it's not every day people walk in your office and claim to be gangsters—and the report came back that he was what he said he was, a member of the Syndicate or whatever you want to call it.

"Okay," I said when Eli came back to the office two days later, "what's your proposition?"

Well, it turned out that he and his associates had been promoting a huge mail order campaign to sell Pega Palo. The Blank Steel Corporation of Chicago had been selling mountains of the drug in the Midwest at prices ranging from $15 to $75 a bottle. But, he said sadly, the Post Office had stepped in. Pega Palo could no longer be advertised or sent through the mails.

"That's one reason I'm here," Eli said. "I want efficacy tests to produce at a court hearing with the Post Office. I want medical proof that Pega Palo is effective. You're going to give them to me."

"Like hell we are," I told him. "Your operation is strictly illegal from our point of view. The Dominican Government has already granted exclusive marketing rights to the Bridges Company."

"Yeah, I wanted to talk to you about that," Eli said, unfazed. "You can tell him from me and my people that he is going to have to do business with us. Otherwise, one day he's going to start his car—and boom. No car, no Bridges."

"Look," I said, "I'm not going to tell the Chief about this, but you had better get the hell out of here. You may run things in Chicago, but we run them here."

That didn't faze him either.

"No, let's be friends. I've been looking around here these last couple of days. The place has real potential. I'd like to bring in 3,000 slot machines, set up special gambling flights from Miami, build a new casino. We'd make this town a second Havana."

"And we can be of help to you in the States," he continued. "You need any guns? No? Well, your boss has lots of enemies; we'd be willing to take care of a few of them— just as a personal favor."

I thanked Eli for his generosity but suggested that he take the next plane out. Otherwise he would leave under police escort. He merely shrugged.

"You want to know something," Eli said as he got up to leave, "I'm going to get those test results. And do you want to know how? I'm going to send down a writer who will do a story for the biggest sex magazine in the U.S. His research will include the tests."

"Thanks for the tip. Your writer will never get out of the airport."

But he did. A few days later Eli wrote me, boldly stating that a story would be run by one of America's biggest adventure magazines. In the meantime, somebody apparently got to the Chief and sold him on the idea that the publicity would be good for Pega Palo sales. The writer turned up, the tests were made and an article was published. By that time, I was sorry I had ever heard of Pega Palo.

A few months later I got a cheery letter from Eli. Sales were booming again, he said, so apparently he had solved his difficulties with the Post Office. Eli even thanked me for my help.

"Remember our plans to make the Dominican Republic a gambling paradise?" he asked coyly. "Well, we will have some of our people contact you in the next few months."

Sure enough, a couple of characters did show up.

They bore, they said, a gift of priceless importance for Trujillo. It was proof, they said soulfully, that we were all buddies. And with great ceremony and trembling fingers they produced a tape recorder.

They played a tape which apparently had been secretly recorded at a clinic in San Juan, Puerto Rico. The clinic had long been known to us as a center of Dominican revolutionary conspiracy, a futile and quite juvenile effort.

So it was no surprise to hear a recording of negotiations between the revolutionaries and the gangsters. The rebels were trying to "sell" the "Dominican gambling concession" for $100,000. Comes the revolution, the rebels promised the gangsters, and you're in.

This is probably the oldest gimmick in the Caribbean revolutionary business. The Cuban and Dominican "gambling concessions" are "sold" over and over again. I told that to our two gangster buddies. I also said that I didn't like their implied threat that they would take their business elsewhere if we didn't play ball.

They were hurt, cut to the quick all during the fast trip to the airport and perhaps beyond. Our agents later reported that the two hoods had indeed bought "revolutionary bonds" which would ensure them their gambling concession. I understand they are still waiting.

All of which proves, I suppose, that there are suckers on both sides of the fence.

Trujillo was, however, a pushover for any deal with a Marine Corps angle to it. He sent several thousands of dollars to a retired Marine in Seattle who called himself Old Sarge. Old Sarge had written Trujillo that he was incurably ill and needed money for medical expenses. An ex-marine on Trujillo's staff pointed out that retired servicemen are entitled to free medical care. The Old Man just shrugged and continued to send money until Old Sarge died.

Another former Marine claimed to have known Trujillo back in the old days. Trujillo didn't remember him from Adam. But that didn't stop the ex-Marine from peddling a fortune in arms to Trujillo at exhorbitant prices. Anything for an old buddy in the Corps!

However, don't get the wrong impression of Trujillo's decision-making ability. He couldn't afford many mistakes. After all he was only a Dominican running that small country with Dominican officials. He had no heaven-sent powers, no vast resources. Yet, he made split-second decisions on almost everything that went on in the country, and most of the decisions worked to his advantage if not to the country's. The people had to be kept reasonably contented, indifferent, or at least not actively hostile. By and large, Trujillo succeeded in this.

Another unique feature of the Trujillo regime business technique was its carefully controlled corruption. The term "corruption" brings to mind a government in which politicians tap the public till amid general confusion. That was not true of Trujillo's government—nobody dared tap Trujillo's till.

The least attempt at graft was swiftly punished. As a matter of fact, the Old Man took pride in the enforced honesty of his officials. He liked to sneer at the Cuba and Venezuela of Batista and Perez Jiminez, where grafting bureaucrats did everything but haul off the capitol buildings.

Things were different in the Dominican Republic. There, only one man took graft—and he was named Trujillo. Like everything else he did, Trujillo's corruption was well organized and of epic proportions. There was, for instance, the famous "10%." This was the amount kicked back to Trujillo on *all* government contracts. If a construction company made a bid to build a road or bridge, the 10% kickback was automatically figured into cost.

Actually, of course, this was not too bad by Latin American standards. In Venezuela under Perez Jimenez, kick-backs of 100% of the real cost were not too uncommon. As I say, that sort of thing made Trujillo feel rather smug and complacent about his own deals.

On the other hand, one of his ugliest fund-raising techniques was his system of crop monopolies, most important of which were in cocoa and coffee. Next to sugar, the two products are the Dominican Republic's most important exports.

So Trujillo took them over. By government decree, Dominican cocoa and coffee producers had to sell their crops through an official monopoly. This enabled the government to set a ridiculously low price for the producer and export the crops at the far higher world prices. Both monopolies netted Trujillo millions of dollars a year.

The Old Man was a businessman of considerable talent, although the fact that he eliminated all business risks may have had something to do with it. When, for instance, he bought a piece of property on speculation, his speculation always paid off. He would sell the property to the government for a high price, buy it back for nickles and dimes, then sell it back to the government for another big chunk. Trujillo would buy and sell the same property over and over again.

Another big source of income was Trujillo's *Partido Dominicano*, Dominican Party, the country's only political party. Nearly every adult Dominican was a member, whether from conviction, necessity or fear. All government employees contributed 10% of their income to the party. And, of course, the party was Trujillo.

Trujillo employed countless other similar fund-raising techniques. He took a share of just about every major enterprise in the republic and any time a new venture was launched, it was never clear whether it belonged to the Old Man or to the government. If the enterprise showed a profit it was Trujillo's; if it failed, it belonged to the government.

So, in one way or another, Trujillo ran the country like
a corporation president who is also majority stockholder.
Trujillo literally owned, as well as ruled, the Dominican
Republic.

In fairness, however, it must be pointed out that Trujillo
himself generated most of the wealth that he stole. When
he took over in 1930, there was literally nothing to steal.
Both the country and its government were completely
bankrupt. But over the years, Trujillo built up a commercial empire which I would estimate was worth about $300,-
000,000, not the $800,000,000 or one billion dollars some
people have reported.

Another myth is that Trujillo salted away hundreds of
millions of dollars in Swiss banks. This is simply not true.
The Old Man never for a moment considered fleeing the
country. His wealth was ploughed back into his most profit-
able Dominican ventures—ventures which sometimes
netted him 300% yearly on his initial investment. A few
million dollars were banked in Canada. However, much of
that money was withdrawn and returned to the Dominican
Republic during the financial crisis of the last years of his
regime.

But the Trujillo heirs had a different financial philosophy.
From the Old Man's death in May, 1961, until the flight of
the last of the Trujillo's the following November, the clan
shipped out almost everything that wasn't nailed down.
I would estimate that all the little Trujillos and their sycho-
pants got away with a total of eighty to a hundred million
dollars.

Here again, wildly exaggerated figures are frequently
mentioned. However, there were simply never such huge
amounts of cash around to steal. The Dominican Republic
is a small agricultural country and that kind of capital just
wasn't available—it being, in addition, rather difficult to
bank a cattle ranch or sugar plantation. In any event, a
hundred million dollars is a respectable haul.

7

Trujillo and Haiti

PORT-AU-PRINCE, capital of Haiti, was second only to Washington as an object of Trujillo's attention. For centuries, Dominicans and Haitians have battled each other on the small island we share. Like most Dominicans, Trujillo feared that the Dominican Republic would eventually be overwhelmed by the greater numbers of the impoverished, illiterate and overcrowded Haitians.

Another very real threat was that Haiti might become a base for anti-Trujillo revolutionaries. So the Generalissimo could never resist trying to manipulate Haitian politics. Neither could the U.S. State Department.

Trujillo money and support, for instance, made Elie Lescot president of Haiti in 1941. The State Department unmade Lescot in 1946. The U.S. Embassy in Port-au-Prince quietly passed the word to the Haitian Army and business community that Lescot had had it so far as Washington was concerned, that Lescot had to go. That was all it took back in those days. The army booted him into exile.

In 1956, however, a third force began to dabble in the Haitian political scene: Cuban revolutionaries. Dr. François Duvalier, at that time a fairly obscure politician and physician, made a deal with ousted Cuban President Carlos Prio. Duvalier needed Prio's help in overthrowing the Haitian government. In return, Duvalier promised the rebels that they could use Haiti as a base of operations against Cuban strongman Fulgencio Batista.

It was a deal. Cuban rebel bomb experts slipped into

Port-au-Prince and began a sort of revolutionary Point Four program. The Cubans gave the Haitians technical aid and instructions in the techniques of sabotage and terrorism. The bomb experts worked with Duvalier henchmen, Clement Barbot and Daniel Francis. (It is interesting to note that Duvalier turned on virtually all his loyal followers once he did get in power. Francis, for instance, was seized, heavy weights were tied to his body, and he was dumped into the Bay of Gonaves. Barbot lasted much longer. For a while Duvalier's most loyal henchman, Barbot, became his most dangerous enemy. Barbot was finally shot to death by Duvalier militia in July of 1963.)

Duvalier launched his bomb campaign in December, 1956. The government promptly collapsed. That didn't mean, however, that "Doc" Duvalier automatically moved into the Presidential Palace. He needed money to buy off the Haitian army. Moreover, Duvalier was confronted by powerful opponents. The upper class, merchants, Catholic Church and U.S. Embassy were supporting the presidential claims of the wealthy Louis Dejoie, an almost-white member of Haiti's so-called elite.

We watched developments closely. In the spring of 1957, Trujillo dispatched a special agent to Port-au-Prince. An American, his mission was to survey the situation and recommend who would be the best man, from Trujillo's point of view, to become president.

The agent conferred secretly with Duvalier and other political leaders. He studied the situation. Duvalier swore undying friendship for Trujillo and promised that he would never permit Haiti to become a base of revolutionary operations. That meant absolutely nothing, of course.

However, Duvalier did display cold political realism. It was evident that he knew that his interests as president would coincide to some extent with those of Trujillo. No more than the Generalissimo could Duvalier afford to have a powerful enemy on the other end of the island. Other Haitian leaders didn't seem to grasp that fact.

There was one other key point which most outsiders and upper-class Haitians themselves had underestimated: that Haiti is about 99% black, and that Haitians had become suddenly aware of the fact. Always, they had been dominated by the mulatto elite which Dejoie represented. Our agent predicted the country would explode in racial violence if Dejoie took power. He fingered Duvalier as the next strongman of Haiti and one with whom Trujillo could do business.

But the Chief was reluctant to commit himself to all-out support of "Doc" Duvalier. The Haitian leader was a civilian. The Generalissimo preferred to deal with military men. Moreover, there were Duvalier's past associations with leftists and his present liaison with the Cuban rebels.

A compromise was made. The Old Man would not oppose Duvalier's bid for power. Token financial support would be made available. Trujillo would then wait and see how Duvalier behaved.

As it turned out, Duvalier didn't need our money. A Cuban rebel named Themistocles Fuentes turned up in Port-au-Prince. He told Duvalier that Fidel Castro and Prio would bankroll Duvalier's election campaign. And they did. The "campaign" consisted of buying off the army and importing hordes of peasants to demonstrate in the streets of the capital. Duvalier was in.

The Old Man watched dubiously as Cuban rebels swarmed into Haiti. Port-au-Prince seemed on the verge of becoming another Miami. Then Duvalier acted. His policy changed overnight. Haitian police scooped up Themistocles Fuentes and his cohorts. Some they dumped into prison, others into the sea. That was the end of Duvalier's flirtation with the Cuban revolutionary movement.

The switch was partly due to fear of Trujillo, partly

because of mathematics. Duvalier's arithmetic went like
this:

Castro and Prio had given him about $200,000 in order
to use Haiti as an anti-Batista base. So Batista offered Duvalier $4,000,000 as a counter-bribe. Duvalier actually re-
ceived only about a million dollars from Batista, but he
couldn't complain; this was par for the course.

By now, you should agree with me that Haitian politics
can be complex. Everybody involved is constantly switching sides.

So, it was now Trujillo's turn to pull an about-face. Duvalier had barely had time to set up housekeeping in the
Presidential Palace before Trujillo had decided he preferred another occupant: Gen. Antoine Kebreau, chief of
the armed forces. The Generalissimo had nothing in particular against Duvalier. He just naturally preferred military men as foreign allies. And I think the Old Man was
a little bored. He liked to stir up his neighbors from time
to time.

Now I was a personal friend of this Kebreau. We had
met years ago at Advanced Infantry School at Fort Ben-
ning, Georgia. Kebreau, who was very black, felt the lash
of discrimination. I was about the only friend he had at
that camp.

So, naturally, I was delegated to suggest to my old buddy
that he should change his title from General to President.
I went over to Port-au-Prince and found that Kebreau
didn't need much urging. Antoine's aspirations were further inspired when I pinned the Dominican Republic's
highest award on his blouse.

"If you need any help in moving into the Palace," I told
him, "you know whom to ask. The Generalissimo will give
you unlimited support."

Kebreau thought it would be nice to hear that from the
Old Man himself. So I invited him to make an official visit
to Ciudad Trujillo. Antoine immediately agreed.

Trujillo received him with all the honors due a chief of state. Kebreau was even addressed as "Mr. President." That did it. Antoine would grab the Palace as soon as he returned to Port-au-Prince. He would be in constant contact with me.

Well, Kebreau's first, and only, request when he returned to Haiti was for a doctor—a Dominican doctor. He didn't trust Haitian doctors. Kebreau had become very ill. Duvalier had put a voodoo hex on him. That's right, a voodoo hex.

Believe it or not, this tough Haitian general curled up his toes and went into a state of shock when Duvalier let him know that he was being hexed. Would-be kingmaker Espaillat was frantic with frustration. I tried everything; so did the doctor we sent to him. It was no use. Finally, Duvalier had Antoine hauled onto a plane and flown to France, where he died.

Trujillo took it philosophically. He called in the Haitian Ambassador. With a straight face, he told the ambassador that he was delighted with Kebreau's fall. The Old Man said he deplored "that some nonsense had taken place between Kebreau and one of my generals."

Duvalier, who had known what was going on all along, and who was every bit as cynical as the Chief, replied that he was also happy that the nonsense was ended. He thanked Trujillo for his good wishes.

In truth, each man now needed the other's support. The Caribbean revolutionary movement was gaining momentum. As early as 1958, a Castro-backed revolutionary offensive against both governments began to take shape. The first shots were fired late in July, 1958.

On July 9, eight men boarded a battered white fishing boat, the *Mollie C*, at Marathon in the Florida Keys. Skipper of the 44-foot craft was Capt. Joe Walker, a tough, aging ex-convict. Walker's mate, Lee Kersten, was also an ex-con. In contrast, there was young Dany Jones. Jones was a Florida deputy sheriff. With him was Bob Hickey, a Miami store manager.

Rounding out the crew were three men with pale-yellow complexions: Capt. Alix Pasquet, late of the Haitian Army, and his brother officers in exile, Philippe Dominique and Henri Perpignand.

Pasquet shared command with Arthur Thomas Payne, a tough and money-hungry Miami deputy sheriff. Payne's ambition was to take over the public relations account of post-revolutionary Haiti. This was getting the account the hard way, but it was the only way Payne knew.

The men finished stowing gear and supplies. Payne discovered a bottle of whiskey somebody had smuggled aboard. He tossed it overboard. The *Mollie C*'s ancient engine began to throb. Payne glanced around, then signaled Walker. Kersten cast off the line and the boat slowly headed out into the Gulf stream. Its destination was Haiti. The mission of the eight-man army was nothing less than the overthrow of the Duvalier government.

This ambitious project, the outcome of which I will describe later, precipitated a half-dozen different investigations. Several U.S. government agencies began probing. Our Miami agents were instructed to investigate. Even the Miami city government launched an inquiry.

The first investigations by city of Miami officials dribbled away into nothing. There was more than a hint that the investigators became progressively less enthusiastic the deeper they probed. It later developed that at least one sleuth assigned to the case had himself been involved. Dissatisfied, the City Manager's Office of Metropolitan Dade County (Miami) retained a former FBI agent, Charles J. Mathews, and turned him loose.

Mathews did his job well—too well. He traced the involvement in the conspiracy of an incredible number of Miami residents, policemen and deputy sheriffs, jewel

thieves, gunrunners, mobsters, gambling syndicates, homo-
sexuals, *bolita* operators, killers, Cuban rebels, even Bahamian politicians. What Mathews uncovered was more than
the workings of another revolutionary conspiracy. His report kicked the top off the teeming anthill that is Miami's
Caribbean underworld. It revealed that catering to Latin
violence is a major Miami industry.

Special Investigator Mathews submitted a 164-page report, was thanked, paid a $5,000 fee, and immediately dis-
missed. The report was suppressed the day it was received.
Federal authorities were equally unenthusiastic about their
copy of his findings. They had reason.

Mathews reported that informants asserted the State
Department had been aware of the planned invasion and
approved of it. A "Confidential Report" submitted to Mathews stated: "the State Department was in possession of
information concerning the revolt ten days before it happened. On July 27, 1958, a State Department official questioned several deputies in the sheriff's office; he was then
advised to lay off." The reason, allegedly, was "because
Duvalier was not cooperating."

The Miami invaders landed in Haiti next day. About 4:30
in the afternoon of July 28th the *Mollie C* chugged into the
seaside village of Deluge, some 50 miles north of Port-au-
Prince and five miles from the town of St. Marc. Walker
nosed his boat alongside the rickety wharf and the Americans jumped ashore. Pasquet, Dominique and Perpignand
remained hidden below deck.

A crowd of villagers swarmed onto the dock to stare at
the newcomers. Among them was the local Chief of Section,
a sort of rural peace officer. Through an interpreter, Payne
told the Chief of Section that the Americans were yachts-
men who had developed engine trouble. They were out of
fuel and water and they wanted to go to Port-au-Prince.

The chief shook his head. The Americans would have to

get permission from the garrison commander at St. Marc, he said. Payne ignored him. The Chief of Section slipped away silently and sent a messenger to St. Marc.

Hours passed while Payne struggled vainly to secure transportation. He was still dickering for a taxi when a battered pickup truck rumbled into the village. Haitian Army Lt. Fenelon Leveille and two privates climbed out. They stared at the Americans, then moved onto the boat deck.

Payne, startled, began a rapid-fire explanation through the interpreter. They were an American fishing party; they had run out of fuel; they now wanted to get back to their Port-au-Prince hotel. . . .

The lieutenant beamed and nodded. Sure, he said, the Americans were free to leave, after their baggage was inspected. A mere routine, of course, but one is compelled to comply with regulations. He prodded at the heaped-up bundles Kersten had already unloaded. The Americans froze as another soldier overturned a crate. Three automatic carbines clattered out on the planking.

Payne didn't hesitate. He plucked a .38 from his waistband and shot the soldier through the head. Pasquet suddenly jerked open a cabin door and fired a machine gun into the crowd. The lieutenant, the other enlisted man and two civilians were chopped down. The villagers fled into the night.

This changed the invaders' plans. By dawn the whole country would be alert and there would be no chance secretly to seize the airfield and await airborne reinforcements.

Payne and his cohorts would have to put back to sea immediately or take a desperate gamble.

If the invaders could seize Caserne Dessalines, the yellow stucco barracks in Port-au-Prince, they might still win. Payne and his men could hold the barracks while Pasquet aroused the underground by phone. Dessalines Barracks is only 200 yards from the rear of the National Palace. They could put the Palace under fire. With luck, they'd have Duvalier fleeing for the hills before morning.

Minutes later the decision was made and the expedition was racing through the darkness toward the capital. Pasquet drove. Two hours later their small truck wheeled down the road past the airport and into the park-like Champs de Mars. On one side, the Palace loomed large and dirty-white. On the other was the brownish-yellow barracks, one gate lit brightly by a floodlight. It was the East Gate, Post No. 1 of the guard.

Pasquet gunned the engine. He roared up to the gate at sixty miles an hour, then slammed on the brakes. The sentry stepped forward and challenged them uncertainly. Somebody flattened him with a rifle butt and the truck lurched into the barracks yard. The invaders tumbled out, shooting wildly.

Leading the invaders into the barracks, Pasquet headed straight for the Adjutant's office. He flung the door open. The duty officer, Lt. Maurice Champagne, was frantically buttoning his trousers when Pasquet cut him down with a tommygun.

The bluff almost worked. Duvalier, panicky, prepared to flee to the Colombian Embassy. For nearly two hours he and his aides were paralyzed by indecision. The occupants of the Palace and the Barracks merely stared silently at each other's buildings. Then the invaders committed a slight tactical error: they sent out for cigarettes.

One of the prisoners was released and told to get cigarettes. "If you don't return," the prisoner was told, "we will kill you." The prisoner was actually on his way back to the barracks with the cigarettes when he changed his mind. He went to the Palace instead. There are only eight men in the Barracks, he told Duvalier.

That did it. Duvalier snapped out of his trance. He clapped a steel helmet on his head, strapped on a web belt and shoved a .45 into the holster. A special squad of couriers was ordered to fan out through the city. They were to summon Duvalier's private party, the several thousand ragged militiamen who had terrorized his enemies for more than a year.

Meanwhile, Pasquet was struggling frantically with Port-au-Prince's chaotic telephone system. Clutching a list of names and numbers, Pasquet sweated while he dialed number after number. He couldn't get through. The city's lines were still torn up. In 1956, Magloire had started to overhaul the system but his government was ousted halfway through the job.

The phone numbers were useless to Pasquet. (Later Duvalier was to find the list fascinating when it was snatched from Pasquet's dead fingers. Few prominent Haitians escaped the ensuing purge.)

Once the bluff had failed and Pasquet had been unable to arouse the underground, the invaders knew they were finished. Duvalier's militiamen poured Stengun fire into the barracks. Payne and his men could do little more than hug the deck.

The end came swiftly in the early dawn. Payne, Perpignand, Hickey and Kersten tried to cut their way out of the trap. They were butchered. Hundreds of militiamen swarmed into the barracks and massacred the remnant. "Payne was the last to die," a militia officer said later. "He was lying under the statue of Jean Christophe. He kept screaming at us: 'Journaliste! Periodiste! Journaliste!'"

"Journalist!" snorted Duvalier a day or two later, "Journalist with a machine gun." The Haitian President's usually impassive face twitched with fury. His anger was directed less at Payne's last words than at the American Embassy attaché who had just made a startling discovery. On inspecting the bodies of the invaders, the attaché had noticed that the blood around Dany Jones' wounds was still fresh. Apparently Jones had been taken prisoner, then shot to death later.

The Haitian president was in no mood to discuss the time of Jones' death. He ordered the attaché expelled. Then Duvalier booted out the Embassy's number two man, the political officer. The Haitian government made it plain that it considered the invasion a Dejoie plot carried out in connivance with U.S. authorities. An immediate investigation was demanded.

The U.S. Embassy fervently agreed that an investigation was in order. It was confused and "dismayed" by contradictory reports from Miami, reports indicating that authorities there had known all along about the invasion conspiracy—had known and done nothing to stop it.

A chief Miami law enforcement official admitted that his men had had the expeditionaries under constant surveillance. Detectives had even trailed the men down to the Keys and observed their embarkation aboard the *Mollie C.*

"Through the early stages of the investigation," the man said, "we thought the deputies were involved in gunrunning. We had no idea that two or three men would be foolish enough to try to overthrow a government." Then he made some countercharges.

"We notified all federal agencies that might possibly be interested," he said, referring to the fact that no warning had been passed on to the Haitians during the expedition's 18 days at sea. "If there was any notification that should have been made to a foreign power, it would have been up to the Federal authorities and not the local police department." The Feds had no answer to that.

The State Department announced that it was investigating through "diplomatic channels," then was silent. Port-au-Prince continued to clamor for the investigation, then it too fell silent. The city of Miami then found itself in the extraordinary role of studying the involvement of American citizens in a international conspiracy aimed at a foreign power.

The probe began within days after the massacre at Dessalines Barracks. The outline of the conspiracy was fairly clear.

It had begun in late 1957 when Payne met Pasquet at a cocktail party. Pasquet was scouting for local gun talent and Payne was rugged and ambitious. Pasquet promised him Haiti's public relations account when they dumped Duvalier. The pair was plotting revolution before they'd downed the last highball.

Payne took to conspiracy like a Cuban university student. But he was still very new and impetuous. On March 28, 1959, the Haitian police marched him to the Port-au-Prince airport and pushed him aboard a Miami-bound plane. "And don't come back," they told him. Payne had been nosing about conspiratorial circles in the Haitian capital. It was to have been a pre-invasion reconnaissance. Payne, ever eager, had fumbled his cover as news photographer and led Duvalier's cops straight into a string of secret conspiratorial cells.

The disaster merely whetted Payne's appetite for direct action. Back in Miami, Payne promptly began to raise his invasion force. One of his first recruits was his close friend and former next-door neighbor, Robert F. Hickey, 35, father of two sons. Then came Dany Jones, the bright young deputy from Titusville, Florida. Payne also lined up four uniformed patrolmen, but all four backed out at the last moment.

The officers later said they had been hired to guard rebel leaders seeking to return to Haiti. Payne had been vague, until it was time to board the *Mollie C*, on the exact circumstances of the return. The officers had been promised $2,000. Then their reward was reduced to $500. By the time the invasion was ready to go the men were helping to finance it out of their own pockets.

Walker and Kersten had also been promised big rewards. Walker was to get $12,000 for the hiring of his boat alone. Dany Jones had been told he was to earn a quick fortune; but Jones' last financial transaction had been to borrow a thousand dollars to contribute toward the cases of M-1's, automatic carbines, tommyguns and pistols, which were loaded aboard the *Mollie C*. Bob Hickey had also mentioned the fabulous profit he expected from a "lobster raising" expedition. Only one of the invaders was making money out of the conspiracy: Payne.

Investigators discovered that Payne had established a second identity for himself, an identity drawing a substantial weekly salary. Detectives found that Payne and Pasquet were in contact with Cuban rebel groups as well as with the Haitian exiles in New York. It was also discovered that a plane, seized the day after the *Mollie C* force was wiped out, had been intended to reinforce Payne's party.

The plane, parked at Miami International Airport, was being loaded with arms when the police moved in. Seventeen men were arrested. Significantly, most of the group were Cubans, members of the 26th of July movement, not Haitians or Dominicans. The arrested men had at first claimed they planned to invade the Dominican Republic.

Investigators were able to reconstruct the invasion plan. Payne's operation had never been intended to execute the coup on its own. It was merely the spearhead. The *Mollie C* force was to have slipped into Port-au-Prince and seized the airport. Simultaneously, the invaders were supposed to have established contact with the underground and triggered an uprising. Then the Palace was to have been attacked. Meanwhile, the planeload of reinforcements was readied in Miami to be rushed to Port-au-Prince on signal. Two other troop-carrying planes were based in New Orleans and may have gotten as far as Jamaica before they turned back.

The unexpected arrival of an army truck and Haiti's

incredibly fouled-up telephone system were all that blocked a major invasion and revolution. Haiti might have fallen to Castro even before Cuba.

Castro later made another attempt to get revenge. On August 13, 1959, an Algerian soldier of fortune, Enrique Fuertes, led a 30-man Cuban force in an invasion of Haiti. The invaders had been told before leaving Cuba that hundreds of armed Haitian rebels were already fighting in the hills. The landing of Cubans was to be the signal for the uprising of another 5,000 guerrillas.

There may have been a ghostly chuckle from the graves of Payne and his cohorts. Like them, the Cubans were slaughtered. But in one sense Payne's group may have been more fortunate; they, at least, were buried. The Cubans were eaten by armed and hungry Haitian peasants. Army patrols found only their blood-stained uniforms.

If there is a moral to the Duvalier story, it is this: in our countries, people like voodoo practitioners and cannibals are as potent in affairs of state as any trained diplomat. They know how to fight and survive in our political jungles. Outsiders—like the Central Intelligence Agency, with all its trained personnel, equipment and lavish budget—do not.

Trujillo and the
United States

ANOTHER editorial boobytrap, I mused, staring at the latest of countless interview questionnaires sent to the Old Man from the American press. Trujillo usually forwarded them to me for appraisal. I checked for loaded questions—questions so cunningly phrased that they made you want to confess to mass homicide—and suggested answers. The Chief would then look over my proposed replies. Usually, he wouldn't bother to change a comma. Other times, he fretted endlessly over terminology and phrasing. When that happened, we ended up with a sometimes startling blend of the prose style of Trujillo and Espaillat. One time we produced a letter to various U.S. Chambers of Commerce which caused quite an unintentional splash.

That letter was merely a forlorn effort to undercut the violent anti-Trujillo publicity campaign in the U.S. The Chambers of Commerce were given an estimate of the amount of products produced in their area which were exported to the Dominican Republic. The letter, ostensibly from the Dominican Chamber of Commerce, suggested that the anti-Trujillo propaganda was threatening that trade. Unfortunately, the letter went out just before the 1958 U.S. elections. We got a fast reaction.

Our letter was immediately construed as an attempt to *influence* the elections. It was bitterly denounced in the U.S. Congress, by various politicians running for office, and by hundreds of newspapers. The State Department also got into the act; it, too, loudly denounced our little epistle. The backfire may have shaken the Chief a bit. The letter had been his idea. However, the Old Man could never resist trying to address himself directly to the American public.

So the trick was to screen out questionnaires and questions which might inspire the Chief to plant his foot in his mouth. That wasn't much of a problem with most queries from the press. The opposition rarely tipped off the newspapers to anything really new. The usual charges of murder and kidnapping would be automatically answered with the usual replies. What intrigued me was that most of the publicized crimes were not true, while some of the Chief's truly drastic "measures" were never spotted. The Old Man probably laughed himself to sleep at night.

This particular questionnaire reached the Palace on October 25, 1956. Trujillo turned it over to me. It was from *Argosy* magazine and prepared by staff writer Gene Lowell. Mr. Lowell seemed intent on linking the Chief to an impressive catalogue of global mayhem.

"Will you either confirm or deny that Porfirio Rubirosa, while posing as a glamor figure of the international set, is actually a 'hatchet man,' as has been charged, in direction of a world-wide counter-movement against the Caribbean Legion underground . . . ?"

I thought about it for a moment. Then, a little wildly, I banged out an answer on my Underwood.

"Congratulations. This is the 52nd time this question has been asked me, but this is the first time I will expose Rubi for what he is. Yes, Porfirio Rubirosa's pursuit of well-heeled broads is actually a mere cover for his real role as head of our Anti-Caribbean Legion underground, Boudoir Brigade . . ."

Nuts. I x'ed it out. The Chief wouldn't appreciate it. However, I would think up a new twist to the answer. It

was about time. That question was almost as old as Rubirosa and that's pretty old.

I passed on to the next question:

"You have long been notably a foe of Communism in
Latin America and are known to have engineered and
financed revolutions that overthrew several Red-dominated
governments in Central and South America. . . .

"I have been informed that the explosive materials that
caused the disastrous Texas City holocaust of 1948 were
munitions purchased by you in the United States for use
against Communist forces in Venezuela and placed aboard
a French vessel. Is it true that, to circumvent your coup,
Communist saboteurs touched off munitions before they
could leave port without regard to the horrible tragedy that
ensued?"

Maybe it was only my suspicious nature, but I didn't like
that question. I wrote: "No. I had no 'explosive materials'
aboard the Texas City ship nor involved in any other holocaust." I suspected the next query would link the Chief to
the sinking of the *Andrea Doria* or the Hindenburg disaster.
I was wrong. It involved the Chief with one of the most
spectacular unsolved murders in New York history.

"I am informed that some of the financial manipulations
of the late Serge Rubinstein, New York financier whose
murder in 1955 never has been solved, seriously jeopard-
ized the monetary structure you had succeeded in stabiliz-
ing in the Dominican Republic. This is said to have occurred about the time you made Rubinstein a citizen of the
Dominican Republic while you were a delegate to the
United Nations. Could the situation have been of such
proportions that Rubinstein was liquidated by Dominicans
seeking vengeance?"

I scanned the rest of the questions. Yes, this was it.
Lowell kept angling back to the "liquidation" of Serge
Rubinstein. *Argosy* magazine had obviously been primed

on the Rubinstein bit by that spectacularly well-financed propaganda task force which was besieging the offices of every major newspaper and magazine in New York and Washington. And the Rubinstein case was a natural. Nothing could be proved or disproved. It was good and murky, wonderful raw material out of which to mold a variety of carefully shaped charges.

There had been a slender line of contact between Rubinstein and the Chief. However, Rubinstein never got a chance to do any financial juggling with Dominican money. His real interest in the Dominican Republic was contained in one grandiose proposal he secretly presented the Generalissimo. Dated March 11, 1953, the seven-page document proposed that the D.R. be converted into a sort of Tangier or Switzerland. The transformation was to evolve around a "Dominican Gold Bank" which was to make the country a financial haven for the world's jittery capitalists.

Two million dollars were available for that purpose, Rubinstein said, and all the Republic would have to do would be to amend a few laws. He represented "a syndicate of financial interests," Rubinstein asserted, who were in a position to assure success. The origin of the proposal was not further explained. Serge merely listed his address —814 Fifth Avenue—and unlisted phone number, Templeton 83773.

He was obviously no judge of the Latin American mentality. By creating a mystery, his Dominican contacts would automatically suspect the worst—and did.

From a strictly economic point of view, however, his proposition still seems sound. There can be no arguing with his opening statement that: "In the world of today there is real necessity for a business area providing: (1) a haven for all forms of wealth; (2) a transferable monetary unit based on gold; (3) a healthy overall climate for capital."

"A study," Rubinstein continued, "reveals that the Dominican Republic meets these qualifications. . . ." That was in 1953. No Caribbean or even Latin American country could qualify today.

Rubinstein made it plain that he was primarily interested in dealing with one medium of exchange. "The Gold Bank of the Dominican Republic will provide sanctuary for all types of wealth and personal fortunes . . . particularly gold." He had also acquired the backing of a mysterious syndicate.

Sometime during the Korean War, Rubinstein seems to have conceived his idea of a "Dominican Gold Bank." When the Chief went to New York in 1953, Rubinstein promptly laid siege. Several New York meetings were arranged and Rubinstein sketched out his plan. The Generalissimo, who knew nothing of Rubinstein, was at first impressed. The deal fell through not because the Boss was worried about Serge's reputation as a financial pirate; the Old Man said he would have nothing to do with a coward. He referred the proposal to the Dominican Development Commission and there it ended when Rubinstein refused to reveal the names of his backers.

There was a curious postscript to the Rubinstein episode. In April 1957, *Argosy* magazine published its long-awaited Rubinstein murder story. We had expected to be clobbered. Instead, *Argosy's* conclusion: Serge Rubinstein had been done in by the Reds. That Trujillo might be involved wasn't even mentioned.

I mentioned this oddity to the Old Man and he nodded thoughtfully. Then the faintest frown crossed Trujillo's face. He was slightly disappointed. The Rubinstein elimination had been something of a masterpiece, but Trujillo was being ignored as a suspect.

The reaction was indicative of one side of Trujillo's character. He really enjoyed his image of the sinister, all-powerful dictator. But he had a split personality. The Old

Man was also pathetically, desperately anxious to be accepted and liked by the United States—to belong. Trujillo's loyalty to the States never wavered; he always hoped that someday, somehow, his Washington "friends" and agents would prevail. To this end no effort, no amount of money was spared. And in no other project did he fail so miserably.

Trujillo adored praise from Americans. I'll never forget the time that the Caesar of the Caribbean went all limp and sentimental because he received a fan letter from a little American girl. For weeks he carried the letter, showing it to everyone within range. It began: "I'm a girl thirteen years old and I'm going to school. My parents don't approve of you, but I think you're doing a great job for your country. . . ."

The letter was signed only by a first name and without a return address. If Trujillo could have located the child, he would have showered her with gifts and money.

But others sure knew how to exploit that craving for acceptance! An endless stream of phonies and frauds constantly flooded the Dominican Republic, laying siege to the Palace. Trujillo was particularly a sucker with prominent people and with those who could claim some sort of connection with public figures. I don't recall a single case in which Trujillo came out ahead in his personal relations campaign. But he never stopped trying. And lots of people walked away with big bundles of loot.

A European duke would turn up and leave with a $25,000 "donation to charity." The wife of a U.S. Ambassador would find that the tropical Santa Claus had put a $17,000 diamond brooch from Tiffany's in her stocking. A friendly newsman would leave a Palace luncheon with $10,000 that he didn't find under his plate. Trujillo, whenever possible, handed out the money himself; he didn't want any confusion about where it was coming from.

Occasionally, however, VIPs were invited to take their

bribes in a more subtle way. A special horse race would be staged and the guest would be told to bet on some nag. All the other jockeys in the race would rein back their horses to permit the VIP's horse to limp to victory. The Chief's guests were always enchanted by horse racing, Trujillo style.

But that sort of thing was merely canapes compared to the banquets of greenbacks served Washington officials. No one will probably ever know how many millions passed into the hands and pockets of some U.S. congressmen and State Department officials. In the last five years, particularly, Trujillo acted like he was trying to buy up the whole U.S. government. I would estimate that he showered at least $5,000,000 on those officials—not to mention the cost of providing many of them with beauteous and capable bed partners. Influential Americans who flourished on Trujillo's various forms of bounty numbered literally in the hundreds. (And I doubt that Trujillo's largest ever showed up on their income tax statements!)

It was all wasted, of course. Time and again, I and others on Trujillo's staff pointed out to him that results were zero. The advice was ignored.

Why did Trujillo resort to that sort of thing? There were several reasons. First, that was about the only way he could influence political developments in the United States. Also, Trujillo was accustomed to doing business that way. In the Caribbean, we have handed out bundles of bills to buy, or at least to rent, elements of the Haitian army, police forces, the Cuban armed forces, the Guatemalan secret service, and sundry other institutions. That sort of thing is pretty common in Latin America.

Ironically, the only American official who ever really did anything for Trujillo didn't have to be paid. That was the late multi-millionaire businessman and diplomat, Joseph Davies of "Mission to Moscow" fame. Davies was also sent on a mission to the Dominican Republic, a mission which, as it turned out, enabled Trujillo to perpetuate himself in power.

At the request of President Roosevelt, Davies went down to the Dominican Republic shortly after Trujillo took office. The Old Man's position was still shaky. The country was bankrupt and owed millions of dollars to the United States. Davies' assignment was to survey the Republic's shattered finances and make recommendations regarding U.S. fiscal policy toward the new regime.

Davies was immensely impressed by Trujillo. He recommended that Washington declare a moratorium on debt payments. This would give Trujillo a breathing spell, enabling him to rebuild the national economy—and also entrench himself in power. Davies made the recommendation solely on the strength of his faith in Trujillo. Trujillo did manage to pay off the debt and from then on he and Davies constituted a two-man mutual admiration society.

I heard the whole story of Trujillo's early years from Davies in 1946. I had been assigned as Davies' aide during his visit to the Dominican Republic that year. Davies was lavish in his praise of Trujillo. "So he's made money," Davies said. "Of course he has. The man is a financial genius. If he had been born in the States he would have become president of General Motors."

The Davies episode was a major reason for Trujillo's lavish payoffs to Washington officials. Trujillo always hoped to find another Davies—to clear up political rather than economic trouble—but he never did.

Trujillo's relations with the State Department were never good. There were two separate but related reasons. For the liberals, who had controlled the Department's Latin American policy-making since the 1930's, Trujillo was a murderous military tyrant. Non-liberals were equally antagonized by the Old Man's independence of action. Trujillo was Washington's friend in everything concerning international policy, but inside the Dominican Republic only one man ruled.

American military men got along well with Trujillo. They respected him, seeing in Trujillo the efficient Marine-trained officer that he was. And, of course, unlike the State Department, the American military suffered from no compulsion to muddle in Dominican internal affairs.

These opposed viewpoints sometimes produced strange situations. In 1950, for instance, the U.S. Army sold me some surplus military equipment. I paid cash and the deal was closed. But the State Department then stepped in and refused to permit me to ship the equipment to the Dominican Republic. That sort of thing happened again and again.

Trujillo viewed the United States with mixed feelings: warm admiration and fear. It must be remembered that he had come to power in 1930, a time when most Caribbean countries were little more than U.S. colonies. Washington ruled through Marines or through ambassadors who held more real power than any local president.

So jealously did Trujillo guard his power that Dominicans soon learned that it was best not to get too close to the American Embassy. Trujillo might worry that some sort of power play was taking shape, and Dominicans knew that worrying Trujillo could be fatal.

In all other areas, however, Trujillo's Marine Corps-instilled loyalty to the United States always prevailed. Even while the State Department was beating his ears off with blame for the Galindez disappearance, details of which I will recount later, the Old Man ignored blandishments from the Kremlin.

The first overture was made on January 1, 1958. Khrushchev and Bulganin (Bulganin was still co-dictator) sent New Years greetings to Trujillo and, through him, to the Dominican people. Ever opportunistic, the Reds apparently thought that the strained relations with Washington could be exploited.

Trujillo, who was just as opportunistic, could have also exploited the threat of improved relations with the Soviets, as has practically every other government in the world. By every tenet of Trujillo's Machiavellian approach to politics, he should have made a big fuss over the gesture and fired greetings right back. By his own lights, he should have played both ends against the middle.

But the Marine Corps officer in Trujillo came through. He gave orders to ignore the message. Late that same evening, our Chief of Communications, Col. Guarionex Saladin, called me. Moscow had sent a follow-up message to ask if the first cable had been received. I went to Trujillo. If only out of common courtesy, we should answer, I told him. He shook his head. The order stood. No answer.

I did make a point of letting the U.S. Ambassador know about it. But that was a waste of time. The Soviets, however, were more flexible. Despite the rebuff, the Kremlin continued to make overtures. They wanted to establish trade relations. Again, they were ignored. The overtures ceased when Castro came to power. And then Trujillo was alone, isolated from both great power blocs.

And right up to the end, the swarm of con-men continued to exploit Trujillo's fight for survival: when economic sanctions were imposed against the Dominican government, a claimed spokesman of the International Longshoremen's Association would drop in. Payment of $25,000 a month to somebody in the ILA will guarantee that no Dominican ships or products will be boycotted by the ILA, he told Trujillo. Trujillo paid.

The Old Man once retained Franklin D. Roosevelt, Jr., as "legal adviser" to the Dominican Government. The fee was considerable, and Roosevelt's services almost negligible. But retaining Roosevelt had one positive result: as long as he was legal adviser, Mrs. Eleanor Roosevelt refrained from knocking the Old Man through the host of liberal organizations to which she belonged.

Money wasn't Trujillo's only method of buying influence. Long ago he had noted that sex has an equally universal appeal. He used what we called "semi-senoritas."

The term can't really be translated into English. I guess the closest you can come to it is "half-virgins," if there is such a species. Semi-senoritas referred to lovely girls from good families who had, by some sexual mishap, spoiled their marriage prospects. Some had been bedded by one or another of the male Trujillo's. These were occasionally employed as clerks in the National Palace or other government buildings.

Other semi-senoritas served as companions for visiting firemen. They were not exactly prostitutes. But it was tacitly understood that, if all went well, the girl and the visiting VIP would wind up in bed. Sometimes this was too subtle for U.S. politicians. Here's an example as told to me by Trujillo's "social secretary":

"A State Department official had been flown down, introduced to the Chief and presented to his semi-senorita, a lovely, refined blond. I had a few drinks with the girl and him at the Hotel Embajador, then told him where I could be reached if he needed me for any reason.

"An American friend had invited me to his home for Thanksgiving dinner. My host had hardly begun carving the turkey when the phone rang. It was the visiting official. " 'What the hell kind of a whore did they give me?' he roared over the phone. 'She won't let me.'

"My first reaction was to tell the idiot to go jump in the swimming pool. But there was no point in making still another powerful enemy.

" 'Put the girl on the phone,' I told him.

"Sobbing, the girl told her story. They had no sooner entered his hotel suite when he jumped on her. Frightened, she had fought him off. I calmed her, and asked her to put the pig back on the phone.

"I tried to explain the situation, that she would submit

only to slow and gentle effort. He finally got the point.

" 'But after you get her pants off, you're on your own,' I told him and hung up. What a pig.

"That character had no business in the semi-senorita league. There was a villa outside the city for animals like him. VIPs who went for that sort of thing were taken there and presented with an array of sultry whores. Nero and Caligula would have been proud of some of the Roman-esque orgies held in that villa."

Some of the Congressmen formed lasting attachments with Trujillo's courtesans. One prominent Southern Senator fell in love with one of the Palace girls. She was quickly shipped off to our Washington embassy where she was made readily available. Another semi-senorita was sent to Washington to become the permanent mistress of a New York Congressman.

But sex remained always secondary to cash in Trujillo's technique for winning friends and influencing people in Washington.

In 1957, for instance, Trujillo began to note the growing surge of Communist power in the Caribbean. His warnings to the Central Intelligence Agency and State Department were ignored. So the Old Man decided to take the facts directly to the U.S. Congress.

Through a middleman, Trujillo turned over $75,000 to a powerful Atlantic seaboard senator. So the senator suddenly became intensely alarmed about Red infiltration in the Caribbean. Forthwith, his committee embarked on an "investigation." The senator himself, accompanied by his "bagman" (I think that's the term), made a quick, quiet trip to the Dominican Republic to confer with Trujillo. The senator was told that the full resources of Dominican intelligence would be mobilized to gather data for his committee.

Months passed. From all over the Caribbean, a flood of reports poured across my desk. Thousands of documents were condensed, collated and translated. There emerged a graphic, factual, and in retrospect, entirely accurate analysis of the situation: a point-by-point study of the Castro-Communist designs on our hemisphere.

Well, the senator received the reports, but probably didn't bother to read them. He made a single and very silly speech denouncing those damned Reds. And that was that. That was what Trujillo got for his $75,000. Altogether, payoffs to that one senator totaled about $225,000.

There is an interesting aspect to this particular case: the intelligence reports sent to that senator included an exhaustive analysis of Fidel Castro's background. It clearly traced Fidel's Communist acts and associations from 1947 to the present. Those facts were apparently totally unknown in Washington. Fortunately for Fidel, this senator didn't give a damn about anything but money. He ignored the information. This was 18 months before Castro triumphed—with the support of the U.S. press and State Department—so the senator's greed literally changed history. Now, when it is too late, he frequently sounds off in pious denunciations of the Castro regime.

In a way, of course, this sort of thing speaks eloquently of the innate greatness of the United States. How else can a foreigner explain the survival of a country, some of whose leaders are so inept and corrupt? Trujillo had, for instance, price lists for the purchase of some U.S. Congressmen. An ordinary, run-of-the-mill Representative would cost about $5,000 or less. A few House committee chairmen could be had for about three times that much, depending on the committee. Senators came higher, of course. A chairman of a key committee could run from $50,000 to $75,000.

Those were the figures on one price list we had. The available politicians were listed under code names, female names like Jean, Paula, Mary, and their asking price. The figures were high by domestic American standards, I have since realized, but the Old Man had to pay plenty to get the Congressmen to sound off on his behalf. That was about all they did—sound off. The birds would sing when Trujillo scattered lots of birdseed. But they were quiet as hell when the Old Man really needed their help in his anti-Communist war.

It was a private operator, however, who probably plucked more plums from Trujillo, in the shortest time, and with the greatest of ease, than anybody else in the Old Man's wheeling and dealing career. It took place in mid-January, 1959, when a smiling, balding, owl-eyed individual flew into Ciudad Trujillo. His name was Alexander Guterma ("But my friends call me Sandy"). With him were his sidekick, Bob Everleigh, and Hal Roach, Jr., son of a retired Hollywood film producer.

Another Guterma buddy turned up later. He was the then Dominican ambassador to Cuba, Porfirio Rubirosa.

This foursome had a scheme to save the Caribbean. How? Easy, the Chief could take over the Mutual Broadcasting System and use its hundreds of affiliated radio stations to alert the American public to the truth about Castro and Communism in the Caribbean. This very laudable enterprise could be accomplished for only about $750,000.

Well, few Dominicans or other Latins ever put anything over on the Old Man—at least until May, 1961. But when it came to Americans, of course, the Generalissimo went all limp and trusting. Open a "Who's Who" of the United States and his staff could pick out fifty or more names of famous Americans who had conned millions out of the Old Man. And so it was with Guterma's deal. It went off smoother than the Brinks job.

One of my closest Palace associates endorsed the proposal and negotiated it on behalf of the Boss. I disagreed loudly and strongly with the deal—particularly with Guterma's bland insistence that MBS could become a propaganda outlet without any repercussions—but kept hands off. The deal was consummated. Stock went one way, cash another. Guterma generously gave my colleague a wire recorder for his very own, then flew back to Washington.

On February 14, 1959, Guterma and Robert J. Everleigh, described as Guterma's "man Friday of one-hundred-and-one fiscal schemes and devices," turned up at the U.S. Courthouse on Foley Square to surrender to warrants for their arrest. The warrants had been secured by the New York Administrator of the Securities and Exchange Commission. Technically, the pair was charged with failure to file reports as required by S.E.C. regulations.

Guterma was bubbling with wrath as he faced reporters on the courthouse steps. "This is the biggest outrage by publicity hounds I have ever heard of. This is all a lie, a publicity stunt in which I am the sacrificial lamb."

But Foley Square was only the beginning of the tribulations of Al Guterma. The whole shaky structure of a fantastically complex financial empire disintegrated like a straw hut in a hurricane as the government probed deeper into his past.

The government's action against Guterma was at first based on a charge almost as vague as Guterma's own shadowy activities. The S.E.C. accused Guterma of failing to report myriad mysterious transactions involving American companies and equally obscure international operators—a mysterious Greek tycoon, some Swiss banks, and Guterma.

This gave S.E.C. agents plenty of room to move around in. They were, in fact, soon lost in the financial labyrinths of Switzerland, Tangier, Panama, Monaco, and other international banking havens. Patiently, they sought to trace the Guterma trail through dozens of American companies, amorphous corporate organizations, name changes, transfers, letterhead corporations; through Panama-registered holding companies and Tangier investment houses and inscrutable Swiss banks. It was a trail booby-trapped with every legal and financial maze known to man—"and some," said a weary investigator, "previously unknown."

One of the most impressive features of this maze was the speed with which it was erected. In little more than eight years, Guterma managed to put together a shadowy empire which may well take another eight years to figure out. Investigators will not, however, be able to backtrack the Guterma story to its beginnings.

The trail stretches from Wall Street, Palm Beach, Switzerland, Tangier, and the Caribbean, back to Japanese-occupied Manila; back still further to pre-war China, and is finally lost in the steppes of Siberia and the Russian civil war. One of these days someone will write a best-seller about the guy.

But back to our story: in January, 1959, Task Force Guterma—Sandy, Bob Everleigh, the hapless Hal Roach, Jr.—disembarked in Ciudad Trujillo. By coincidence, Rubi decided to come home. He needed home leave, for life was strenuous in the Cuban capital, what with Fidel shooting a lot of Rubi's old friends. Somebody had also tossed a bomb at him, and besides, Rubirosa wired Foreign Relations, he wanted to attend the annual cattle show being held that month. The Secretary of Foreign Relations was somewhat startled at Rubi's sudden interest in livestock, but he granted him home leave.

Rubirosa worked furiously in Guterma's behalf. He lobbied and buttonholed. He fluttered and hovered around the power-that-was in the Dominican Republic. He projected that high-voltage Rubirosa personality. Rubirosa was at least matched by the stepped-up Guterma charm. Sandy had conceived an overpowering hatred for Fidel; he, as a civic-minded citizen, was lusting for a chance to expose him for what he was. Mutual would do so as a public service. However, Mutual found itself in temporary financial difficulties. . . . it took barely a week.

Rubi went back to Havana. Guterma and his boys returned to New York. They took with them $750,000. They left behind as security a stack of stock certificates. Attorneys who later examined them admired the engraving. Artistically, they were magnificent; financially, they were worthless.

Sandy's empire seemed just as ephemeral when it began to fall apart a month later. The Dominican deal eventually resulted in charges that he was a "foreign agent." The $750,000, however, had vanished—presumably Guterma had squirrelled it away in Switzerland. Investigators turned up no end of overseas leads but without exception failed to follow them up.

Even odder, I think, is the fact that investigators chose to overlook that Guterma did at least appear to live up to his agreement. For a month or two, the Mutual Broadcasting System had indeed presented celebrities who praised the Old Man over MBS.

Following is a transcript of one such broadcast, as published in *The Herald* of the Dominican Republic of February 21, 1959:

Senator Sees Trujillo as U.S. Friend, Scores Castro's Acts

Senator Allen J. Ellender, Democrat of Louisiana, was recently a visitor in Ciudad Trujillo. While here he conferred with Generalissimo Trujillo, President Trujillo and other officials of the Dominican government. He was also invited to address a joint session of the Dominican congress which he readily accepted.

Upon his return to the United States, Senator Ellender was requested to appear on Mutual Broadcasting System's nation-wide program,"Capital Assignment," as guest of honor. The program was aired February 16th. The following is an edited transcript of that broadcast.

Warren: Where were you, Senator?

Ellender: I visited every country in Central America as well as every country in South America with the exception of Bolivia and Paraguay. . . .

Warren: You did get to the Dominican Republic?

Ellender: Oh yes, I did. I had a long conversation with Trujillo and his brother who is now the President and many of the officials who carry on in that Republic.

Warren: Well, which leads me to this question. Senator Ellender, there's been considerable criticism here in the United States of President Trujillo in the Dominican Republic. You were there. Now, how did Trujillo impress you?

Ellender: Well, Trujillo impressed me as being a hard worker. I visited with him before and he is a human dynamo whose energies are being used, as far as I could tell, in order to lift the economic condition of the Dominican Republic.

Warren: Are the people behind him, Senator?

Ellender: Oh, there's no question about that in my mind, for the simple reason that two weeks before I got there, there were over 300,000 people in Trujillo, that is a city—Trujillo—to celebrate his 63rd or 64th birthday-anniversary and I was told by our Ambassador and all of our people there that Trujillo is now beloved by the people of the Dominican Republic because of vast improvements he has made in order to benefit the people of that Republic as a whole.

Warren: As an expression of that, Senator, if they were to have an election in the Dominican Republic, tomorrow—Tuesday—would he, Trujillo, be elected?

Ellender: I have no doubts about that.

Warren: By ballots, or bullets?

Ellender: By ballots—ballots—because Trujillo's work —it has been widespread—and there's not a city or village of any size in the Dominican Republic, I was told by my own people, that hasn't got good schools, hospitals, good streets, sidewalks and the city of Trujillo itself has had its face lifted in the past few years to the extent that it is now a very modern city.

Warren: Is the Dominican Republic, Senator, friendly to the United States?

Ellender: Well, that was the first question I asked of Mr. Trujillo and his brother, the President, and both answered that they don't know what could be done now to improve, or further improve, the good relationship that now exists between the two countries.

Warren: Then, you wouldn't compare Trujillo to Castro in any way?

Ellender: Oh, God no! There is as much difference as night and day between Castro and Mr. Trujillo. . . .

Warren: Judging from Mr. Castro's expressions in the past, say two or three weeks, I don't believe that he is a friend of America at all, the United States, I mean—that he is likely to give us some trouble.

Warren: Who is our best friend in Latin America right now Senator?

Ellender: Well, I don't know. It's pretty hard to say. We've got the President of Argentina—I believe he is a good man. You have the President of Brazil, whom I believe is a good man. You have the President of Mexico, whom I believe is a good man. And I go back to the Dominican Republic. I am not here to discuss in detail how Mr. Trujillo has handled the affairs of state there but I'm for results that were obtained by him. And certainly Mr. Trujillo has done a good job in raising the economy of the people and improving the plight of the people in the Dominican Republic and bringing in there a lot of improvements that are very beneficial to the population.

Warren: Well, thank you very much, Senator. I have

been speaking with Senator Allen Ellender, Democrat of Louisiana. This is Charles Warren, Mutual News, in Washington.

And so it went. Trujillo's dealings with the United States consisted of almost endless skirmishing, open and undercover, on both sides. Trujillo, a political and financial pirate himself, couldn't conceive of operating any other way. Moreover, as will be seen in the next chapter, the piratical nature of Dominican-American relations followed a century-old precedent.

The Piratess
and the Politician

"**O**UR man in Washington is bucking for a hole in the head," I mused, gazing at the pile of papers heaped high on my desk. They were hundreds of photostats of fading documents: contracts, water and mineral rights, railroad and river transportation concessions, real estate deeds and leases—all nearly a century old. I hadn't the slightest idea where the originals had come from. But one thing was obvious. If the documents were legally valid, the Dominican Republic belonged to a very prominent U.S. Congressman. Ironically, the Congressman had repeatedly professed to be a bosom buddy of the Old Man. At least he said so fervently enough when Trujillo's birdseed inspired him to heights of voluble affection. And now that same Congressman seemed to think these documents entitled him to the ownership of the Dominican Republic. No wonder the Old Man had been annoyed; *he* owned the Dominican Republic!

This particular act of attempted Caribbean piracy took place in September, 1960. It began when the Chief called me into his tiny office. I automatically checked his facial expression: his eyes were frozen and curiously colorless, his mouth hard.

He was in a bad mood.

"I want an immediate report on this." The Old Man tapped his fingers impatiently on a stack of documents piled on the chair by his desk. "And take this with you," he added, handing me a letter on his desk. "You figure out what these gangsters are trying to pull."

Back at my desk I read the letter and looked over the documents. They had been sent by one of our Washington agents, a registered lobbyist who operated in a shadowy world of string-pulling, influence-peddling and intrigue both high and low. He was currently on our payroll, but that meant little. If the price were right, he'd arrange for somebody to steal the Washington Monument for you; for somebody else's fee, he'd have stolen it back. He was, in short, a real prize. But he did have amazing contacts. Among other feats, he had been partially responsible for initiating that Congressional "investigation" of Communism in the Caribbean.

In proof of his undying devotion and admiration for the Chief, the lobbyist wrote, and as proof that he merited those crisp bills which reached him regularly in a plain white envelope—our friend was allergic to paying income taxes—he had performed a veritable *tour de force*. It would undoubtedly save the republic from economic ruin. He had, he said, intercepted a bill which was to be presented on the floor of the House within the coming week. Passage of the bill, he warned, would wreak havoc on the splendid progress made in the Era which bore Trujillo's name.

I paused to admire his approach; funny thing, both Americans and Dominicans used the same prose style when trying to pry the Old Man loose from wads of pesos and dollars. But this approach was new. I read on.

He had, our good friend continued, prevailed on the author of the bill to delay his rash action, assuring this distinguished Congressman that it was all a misunderstanding which the Generalissimo would be delighted to rectify. However, he warned, urgency was paramount. Otherwise, his dear and powerful friend would be sorrowfully compelled to initiate action which would abolish the quota permitting Dominican sugar to be sold in the United States.

I read that last part again. It might be serious. In the Caribbean, a threat to wipe out the sugar quota for the U.S. market has rather more impact than threatening to kidnap the wife and kids. That was why Trujillo spent fortunes maintaining a corps of sugar lobbyists in Washington. But it still wasn't clear what this had to do with the stacks of photostats he had sent.

The lobbyist's letter concluded by warning that only prompt restitution of American property expropriated by the Dominican Republic could prevent such a dire catastrophe as that represented by the bill which he had so adroitly snatched from the jaws of the Congressional hopper. He was enclosing, he said, this very same bill. I looked at it.

I had never seen one before, but a Congressional bill it obviously was. It stated merely that whereas the United States sugar quota is a form of subsidy, and that whereas national policy dictates that no aid or subsidy be extended to foreign parties who have taken actions inimical to the national interest, and whereas the Dominican Republic has seen fit to unlawfully seize properties owned by a U.S. firm —the American West Indies Company—the Congress must thus take reprisal by forbidding the sale of Dominican sugar in the United States.

So that was it! The bill was a hoax. In collusion, our Washington agent and the Congressman were attempting a very unsubtle shakedown. As I say, the author of the bill was supposed to be a good friend of the Chief. The Old Man had awarded him the Republic's highest decoration. More meaningful awards were routed to him through his Washington administrative assistant. Well, it wouldn't work. There was enough documentation of the payoffs to that honorable Congressman to have put him behind bars for quite a spell.

(That documentation, incidentally, plus a wealth of other incriminating files, have long since been removed to Washington by the State Department. What will be done with them? You may be sure that some of the most eminent people in the U.S. are also pondering that question!)

I knew, however, that the old Man would want to avoid an open clash, if possible, with his Congressional "friend." I decided to check that so-called American West Indies Company. I'd never heard of it. I was sure that no such company even existed in the Dominican Republic, let alone had been expropriated.

Just then, a young captain walked in, saluted and handed me another letter. "The Chief says you are to take care of this, too. It just came in." I opened it. On plain white paper, the typewritten letter carried a Boston office building as return address. It was signed by the Congressman of the sugar bill, our friend. It was addressed to his good friend Generalissimo Trujillo.

It was, naturally, a friendly letter. The Congressman made no mention of the sugar bill. He merely indicated that he and some associates were interested in the American West Indies Company and that said company had somehow been done out of its holdings in and around the city of Azua in the Republic. He cited dimensions of the property in the area. His claim totalled about a half million acres. He would, the Congressman said, appreciate its return. He was sure it was all a mistake. Documents had already been forwarded which attested to the company's ownership.

Now the light dawned. By extraordinary coincidence the American West Indies Company's claim roughly corresponded to the Azua oil concession. Petroleum geologists had a theory that the fabulous Maracaibo oil basin extended far out under the Caribbean, extended all the way to the Azua region of the Dominican Republic. Drillers were already hopefully sinking holes deep in the area.

I turned to the heap of documents which were supposed to prove that our good Congressional friend had the right to tap the Maracaibo millions. I expected something like the Spanish Royal land grants which are still being manufactured and sold, giving you kingly authorization to large chunks of Colombia or Bolivia at bargain basement prices. Curiously, the century-old documents seemed not only genuine, but indicated that the American West Indies Company owned most of the Dominican Republic.

There were scores of deeds, each covering huge tracts of land in virtually every section of the country. It seemed the Dominican Republic was now a fief of a corrupt, powerful Washington politician.

But who or what is or was the "American West Indies Company?" The present claimants to the company's apparent holdings seemed to have only the foggiest idea of what was involved. I turned to the documents and began to read. Later, I sent for history books from the National Archives.

I found that the American West Indies Company is the story of a nineteenth century she-politician with far more imagination and daring than her modern Washington counterparts. Here is that story. I am including it here, the earliest of the majestic swindles which have worked both ways between the Dominican Republic and the United States. It is the story of Jane Cazneau, piratess extraordinary.

Her contemporaries portrayed her as a striking beauty. She was "at once well bred and disturbingly sensual," one writer coyly remarks. She had a "cameo complexion heightened by cascading black hair."

Jane also had brains to go with her beauty and she had no scruples about using either asset. In her sweetly feminine way, Jane precipitated as much Caribbean violence as Fidel Castro: her dreams of empire sent whole battle fleets across the Atlantic, caused invasions, civil war, military occupation.

Yet she has been lost in obscurity. Jane Cazneau was the confidante of presidents, advisors, and generals. She was a reckless gambler, wagering her own life with entire nations as the stakes. "Beautiful, brilliant," Aaron Burr said of her. "A born insurrector," said her critics. "A terror with her pen," admitted a U.S. Senator who accused her of responsibility for the war with Mexico.

Jane Cazneau was born Jane McManus in Troy, New York in 1807. Her father was a moderately distinguished lawyer and politician who had served a term in Congress. The McManuses were eminently respectable small town gentry. Then along came Jane.

Jane's early life doesn't concern us here. Suffice it to say that she served as an espionage agent in Mexico City during the Mexican War (she tried to annex that country to the United States), backed several Cuban revolutions, married a frontier adventurer named Gen. William Cazneau, and, finally, tried to take over the Dominican Republic. And damned near succeeded.

Her Dominican adventure began in 1854, and for the next decade or so, the activities of the Cazneaus kept the Caribbean in a turmoil. As American envoy and wife, the couple precipitated a war between Haiti and the Dominican Republic. Cazneau intrigues caused British, French and Spanish fleets to mobilize in the Caribbean to block the Republic's annexation to the United States, resulting in constant diplomatic crises.

Then, in 1860, there was an eyeball-to-eyeball confrontation of the United States and the European powers. The U.S. backed down at the last moment and war was avoided, but the bankrupt Dominican government—which had counted on promised U.S. subsidies after annexation—collapsed. The Dominican Republic lapsed into anarchy; famine and plague followed the march of ravaging armies. The population was decimated, the country left prostrate.

The United States was now also torn by civil war. There was now no danger that the U.S. would annex Santo Domingo, so the British and French lost all interest in our country. Only the Spaniards were left. At the invitation of the Dominican government, the red and gold banner of Castillo and Leon was again hoisted over the National Pal-

ace. The Dominican President became a Spanish royal vice-
roy.

The Cazneaus didn't even blink at this turn for the
worse. There is always more than one way to take over a
country. They decided to buy up Santo Domingo, piece by
piece. The U.S. Civil War was raging, but the Spaniards,
ever nervous about Cuba and Puerto Rico, were eager to
please the ever-insistent American envoy. If he and his
charming wife could be kept happy by being deeded
chunks of land the Spanish didn't even own . . . Well, he was
ready to oblige.

This is how the American West Indies Company was
"founded." The Cazneaus entered into a partnership with a
Col. Joseph W. Fabens, another Caribbean fortune hunter.
While Jane turned out glowing brochures on the delights of
settling in the tropical paradise that was Santo Domingo,
William and Fabens happily set about drawing up an almost endless series of land contracts. Obscure Spanish officials scrawled elaborate rubrics, for a small fee, across the
bottom of the English language documents which Cazneau
put before them.

Cazneau also proposed to "establish a current of immigration." In return for this he asked for the exclusive privi-
lege of shipping on the country's two largest rivers, a concession to establish a shipyard, "exploitation of the coal
mines and all other mines of the Republic," and huge tracts
of land for his "agricultural colonists."

He acquired most of these concessions over the years;
he occasionally failed, but this didn't stop Cazneau from
claiming everything in his advertising and promotion.

The American West Indies Company was formed in New
York in 1862. Jane Cazneau wrote a glowing prospectus
which extolled the site of the colonies in glittering general-
ities:

"The land has the reputation of being one of the most
beautiful and healthful spots on the south side of the is-

land," wrote Jane between bouts with malaria. "The example and instruction it will afford to other settlers will be of incalculable value to those while constituting the best mode of employing the best classes of free labor in a manner which will insure permanent homes and satisfactory means of livelihood. . . ."

Immigrants flocked to the island by the hundreds. Few left. Most of them stayed right in Santo Domingo, *buried* in those "beautiful and healthful spots." Unused to the climate, the fevers, the primitiveness, they perished like victims of a plague. An American businessman, resident in the Republic at that time, later gave an account of the "colonization" scheme:

"Upon an investment of short of $4,000 in wild lands in Santo Domingo, Cazneau and Fabens represented that they had property to the value of $2,000,000—the capital of the company. They sacrificed hundreds of lives by their fake representations; and those that escaped with their lives lost everything. Not one remained. Cazneau and Fabens made small fortunes out of the operation."

The American Commercial Agent in Santo Domingo also gave a vivid description of the surviving immigrants who fled the country "cursing in their hearts the West Indies Company of Fabens and Cazneau."

The Cazneaus' colonists may have been wiped out by the hundreds, but the couple themselves thrived. They grabbed more mineral rights, took a lease on the entire port of Santo Domingo City, founded the National Bank of Santo Domingo, and established a shipping line between Santo Domingo and New York.

This was all in the documents heaped on my desk. There was also mention of a typically offbeat Cazneau project—camels.

It seems that their new partner, Fabens, was a camel enthusiast. He was fascinated by the beasts. Fabens had come across camels during travels in North Africa and Arabia and they became a lifelong obsession. He even wrote a romantic novel in which a camel was hero. Fabens managed to enlist the Cazneaus into his camel fan club.

The trio got involved in a number of obscure camel enterprises. There is even some indication that Jane accompanied Fabens on a camel-buying expedition to Morocco. It is known that he shipped camels to Santo Domingo—where they died even faster than the colonists—and to Texas for use by the U.S. Army. They also seem to have tried to peddle the beasts in Panama and Peru.

The Cazneaus' compulsion to dabble in almost everything that came within range always ended disastrously for the objects of their interest. Humans, animals, governments, causes, nations—all seemed to disintegrate under the Cazneau touch. Jane and William themselves invariably emerged unscarred and somewhat breathlessly innocent. What ultimately proved fatal however, was their involvement in the American Civil War. Fortunately for the Union, Jane and Bill supported the Confederacy.

Their pro-Southern activities were for the most part quiet. There is some indication that they actually served as Confederate secret agents. In January, 1863, the famous rebel raider, *Alabama,* dropped anchor in the roadstead of Santo Domingo City. The *Alabama's* skipper, Capt. Ralph Semmes, was rowed ashore. His first move after clearance by colonial officials was to call at the Cazneau residence, Estancia Esmeralda.

For several months Santo Domingo was the *Alabama's* base of operations. The raider swooped down on one Yankee merchantman after another, ship after ship went to the bottom, and the *Alabama* landed captured Union crewmen in Santo Domingo. The *Alabama's* skipper obviously enjoyed excellent marine intelligence, always knowing when and where to intercept Union cargoes. And he was snugly berthed in Santo Domingo City during those rare occasions that Union cruisers nosed too close.

This was too much for the official U.S. agent in Santo Domingo, the peppery William Yeager. He depicted the Union officers as winding lotus leaves in their hair while the *Alabama* swept the Caribbean. Finally, Washington prodded the languid Caribbean squadron into more vigorous action. Pressure was also put on the Spaniards. The *Alabama* was forced to flee across the Atlantic to France where it was later destroyed. Yeager took personal credit.

"So long as they [the Caribbean squadron] could lay in St. Thomas, and the officers indulge in iced drinks and cocktails," Yeager wrote in a triumphant letter to Secretary of State Seward, "they cared nothing about the *Alabama*."

Long before the end of the *Alabama*, the Cazneaus were also in trouble. Caribbean empire-building and Confederate intrigue had come to an abrupt end in 1863 when the Spaniards suddenly turned on their two American friends. As usual, what happened is unclear. The Spaniards did burn down the Cazneau home and again they were forced to flee. Packing their precious "deeds," leases and concessions in a huge steamer trunk they boarded ship for New York.

(I never found out how that trunk got to Boston; there's probably an interesting story there.)

The Cazneaus would be back. Meanwhile, they would wait out the war by organizing the San Domingo Cotton Company and the San Domingo Company. They sold stock, granted concessions, leased land, and made money. With the exception of the currency, their paper was as phony as their previous transactions.

The Spaniards finally withdrew in June, 1865. The Cazneaus promptly returned. The country was in a shambles, true, but it was under such conditions that the couple thrived. And things were looking up in Washington.

Secretary of State Seward was obsessed with restoring

the shattered Monroe Doctrine—a collapse that had begun well before the Civil War. He believed it vital that the United States acquire a fortified base in the Caribbean. He decided upon Santo Domingo. Weak from the wounds made by Lincoln's assassins, his broken jaw still bound to his head, Seward set sail for Santo Domingo. He arrived January 15, 1866.

Jane and Bill were on the dock cheering when Seward stepped ashore. They escorted him to the Dominican president and about the country with the aplomb of real estate agents in a housing development.

Seward was enormously impressed by the undeniably dynamic Cazneau personality. When he returned to Washington he was followed by rapid-fire high-pressure letters from Jane. The couple hammered away on the desirability of direct annexation. The Secretary became a firm fan of the family.

Just as he appeared to have the White House in his pocket, the Cazneaus suffered another of their heartbreaking setbacks. Their Dominican president was overthrown. Painfully, Jane and William worked the revolutionary party into line.

Then there was still another disaster. Seward nominated Cazneau to be U.S. Minister Resident in Santo Domingo and approval had to be given by Congress. This was the chance Cazneau's enemies—not surprisingly, there was a sizeable contingent of people who made hating Cazneau a lifelong purpose—had been waiting for. They promptly introduced evidence into the Congressional hearings which curled Seward's thinning pelt. Most effective of the charges in post-Civil War Washington related to Cazneau's Confederate sympathies and suspected activities. Seward dropped the nomination, but continued to correspond with him.

On and on dragged the negotiations over the base. Revolutionary armies marched back and forth across succeeding Dominican governments. Seward himself was relieved of his office, his Dominican ambitions still unresolved, in the spring of 1869 with the inauguration of General Grant. Seward stepped out on March 4. By March 9, Cazneau's partner, Fabens, was deep in conference with Seward's successor, Secretary of State Hamilton Fish. Fabens left a memo with the Secretary which bluntly advised that the U.S. Government take "the act providing for the annexation of Texas as a model . . . (and) accept the Dominican Republic as one of its States."

Fabens also began feverishly lobbying with Congress. He enlisted the powerful support of the Chairman of the House Committee on Foreign Affairs. The Cazneaus began churning out reports and promotional material which Fabens showered on the Congressmen. Jane Cazneau turned out one glittering publicity release after another for the *New York Herald* and other powerful newspapers.

Grant selected one of his private secretaries, General Orville Babcock, as his Commissioner in Santo Domingo. Babcock was instructed to "obtain full and accurate information in regard to the disposition of the Government and people of the Republic toward the United States . . ." and generally determine the advisability of annexation.

The Cazneaus were on the dock cheering as Babcock stepped ashore. Whatever the future of Santo Domingo there was no doubt that the Cazneaus had successfully annexed the President's Commissioner. The Cazneaus were present as adviser to Babcock at each conference between the Commissioner and the Dominican President. Jane also graciously consented to act as interpreter. This really speeded up negotiations; both parties were invariably delighted with all conversations routed through Jane.

Before he returned to Washington Babcock cheerfully signed a rather unusual statement drafted by the very fluent Cazneaus:

"Orville E. Babcock, aide-de-camp to His Excellency

Ulysses S. Grant, President of the United States of America, and his Special Agent to the Dominican Republic, contracted and agreed in the name and behalf of the President that he should use all his influence with the members of Congress to popularize the idea of annexing the Dominican Republic to the United States and that he should withhold from them all official communication on the subject until certain of its approval by a majority."

President Grant now pushed for annexation. The Dominican President, eager for the move and the cash allocation which was to be turned over to his government when the treaty was signed, encouraged Cazneau to ever greater efforts. Concession after concession was turned over to them.

Both the American and Dominican presidents treated the Cazneaus almost as sovereign in Dominican affairs. A U.S. diplomat unwisely denounced them as "speculators who stopped at nothing to bring about their own selfish ends." The Cazneaus had him ousted. Many Dominicans were less enthusiastic about becoming one of the United States. Revolutionary conspiracies bubbled over almost weekly.

Cazneau became alarmed at the growing strength of a Dominican rebel army being organized in neighboring Haiti. He called upon Grant to send the U.S. Navy—which he did. By the end of 1870 Cazneau was indirectly commanding a squadron of seven U.S. warships. The frightened Haitians jailed most of the rebels.

Now Cazneau and his Dominican allies turned their attention to the plebiscite which would authorize annexation to the U.S. The Dominican officials thought this a novel idea but went along to humor the Americans. The President assured the electorate that the vote would be free and secret and that anyone could vote against annexation, but they would be shot if they did. Sixteen thousand votes were cast—all for annexation. The officials decided this looked a bit too lopsided: out of respect for the democratic process, they cast 11 votes against it.

That out of the way, the Cazneaus had their President parcel out Santo Domingo. They picked up another 200,000-acre grant, the last of the country's mineral concessions, and other choice bits.

But they were going too far. American critics of the corruption-riddled Grant administration suddenly realized that Santo Domingo had become the personal fief of the couple arranging its annexation. The Dominican President freely admitted the huge concessions that had been made to Cazneau and that Cazneau was to be the first U.S. Governor of Santo Domingo. The scandal quickly boiled over in Congress.

Here was fought the last battle of the years of torturous intrigue. Cazneau's Congressional partisans were vigorous and determined. But confronting them was an equally determined and far more eloquent Senator, Charles Summer. Again and again the proposed treaty seemed on the point of Congressional approval. Each time, Summer and a small clique of allies managed a last minute block.

"The resolution before the Senate," Summer thundered, "commits Congress to a dance of blood. It is a new step in a measure of violence."

Finally and firmly the Senate turned down the proposed treaty to annex the Cazneau real estate empire. It disintegrated.

The Senate's action also finished Jane and William Cazneau. They left the island and vanished into obscurity. Two years later they were reported to have gone down in a shipwreck. All that apparently remained of the Cazneaus was this stack of worthless paper.

"So that is the story," the Chief mused. "I would like to have known that Jane Cazneau . . . you say she was lost at sea? It is unfortunate for our Congressional friend that this didn't sink with her." He gestured at the documents. "He has probably gone to considerable time and expense to secure this garbage. I wonder where he found it. No matter; these papers will do him no more good than they did the Cazneaus and Fabens.

"Here is what you will do. Refer our Washington friend to the Land Courts. Then ignore him. Don't answer any further letters from him. He is intelligent enough, I believe, not to press the issue. Photostat all this and his correspondence and get the address of his hometown newspaper."

"Oh, yes," Trujillo added, turning to another aide, "instruct a Land Court to prepare a bill for the back taxes owed on all that property." Then he turned his attention to the latest intelligence summary from Cuba.

A series of protesting letters from the Congressman sputtered to an end when he received a bill for one billion dollars owed on "back taxes." Our oh-so-clever Washington lobbyist was fired. And that was the end of the second American West Indies Company.

10

"Caribbean Agents"

"YES, my friend," the colonel waved a didactic finger, "I admire your American Intelligence Services for their excellent electronic devices. I have seen those infallible lie detectors, those incredible listening devices, the tiny communications unit you can conceal in the palm of your hand. And, of course, your aerial photography is superb. But, I repeat, you really are old-fashioned."

The colonel was one of my officers, an old friend and colleague and a veteran of years of Caribbean espionage. He was explaining our intelligence methods to a visiting American official.

"When I worked with your people I would bring them huge quantities of reports, rumors, leaks, and scraps of information. They would always ask me: 'Can you *document* this or that report?'

"I would tell them: 'Do you think this is nineteenth century Europe, and that I can bring you the blueprints of a battleship or the secret mobilization plans of Austria-Hungary? This is the Caribbean and this is modern, irregular warfare.'

"Nobody here draws up fancy staff documents and ties them with pretty ribbons. You have to take that mess of information I supply, roll up your sleeves, and try to make some sense out of it.

"You have to say, 'Okay, maybe this story is a plant. If so, why, and who planted it?'

"But you don't say that. You say, 'This looks pretty

phoney to us.' You accept or reject each item on its own narrow merits. Maybe they did that in Europe, but here you have to take every scrap of information, put them all together and figure out the total sum of all those lies, half-lies and half-truths.

"Remember, in Latin countries there are very few absolute, unadorned facts and there is no such thing as absolute morality. Nothing is black or white in the tropics.

"And you always forget that nothing can be kept an absolute secret in these countries. There is always a leak. So what we all do is try to confuse issues by planting endless false leads. We make a smoke screen and hope that we can complete our operation before the opposition figures out precisely what we are up to. Because they will find out eventually. They'll add up all the stories, even our planted ones, and come to a correct conclusion.

"That means we have to work fast. Undercover operations here must be kept simple, even primitive. Yours never are. Your work is always so elaborate, so slow and complex.

"What is dangerous about working with Americans is that your undercover work becomes so involved. There is such a wide dispersal of activities and information. All sorts of people are dragged into the picture.

"Somebody always organizes a complicated system of co-ordination, and consequently information leaks out all over the place. There are endless conferences and elaborate security measures which rarely accomplish anything, except that they attract attention.

"At the same time you often neglect basic *counter*-intelligence. At the Guatemalan camps of the Bay of Pigs exile-troops, for instance, everything was super-secret. But the men in the camp were in contact with their families in Miami. And in Miami there were swarms of known Castro agents. Let me repeat: known Castro agents.

"The Miami police knew the identity of Castro's spies but Washington never took any action against them. So, when the exiles landed in Cuba, Castro had tanks, guns, and planes waiting for them. . . .

"But let me get back to what I mean by 'old-fashioned.' First, this is gutter fighting—right? Like it or not, this means you've got to get down and root in the gutter. But not your people! To them, intelligence concerns government offices and embassies and politicians.

"That is a nice way to operate. But this is a war that's planned and fought in back alleys and mountain caves.

"In these countries a sweaty union agent or a dirty *campesino* is usually more important to intelligence work than an ambassador. Some student leader or intellectual may control more real power than a cabinet minister. A scrubby *cantina* can be more important to you than a national palace.

"No, there is no longer a place for your cloak and dagger operations. Our new garb is a poncho and frayed white cotton work clothes. Espionage has moved out of the diplomatic salons and onto our dusty streets.

"And for that type of work you need a lot of local professionals. But you don't have them. You use Americans. You know how it is in the islands: any American is as conspicuous as a Yukon totem pole. Your spies that come around here stick out like they had two heads.

"How many Russian spies—I mean real Russians—do you think there are here? Very, very few. The Communists are smart. They use trained local nationals.

"You have plenty of retired American military officers and clean-cut young men in your secret services. In fact, you have far too many. You also have some local informants, and almost all are unreliable.

"You don't have a trained corps of intelligent, professional agents native to the region in which they serve. Why, few of your CIA organizers of the Cuban invasion could even speak passable Spanish!

"Worst of all, your agents come charging in like the Light

Brigade. They're so obvious that they frighten people away, people who'd like to help them.

"How often your two-headed spies have led the Communists straight to local undercover organizations! You sent Yankee electronic experts into Havana and helped wipe out half the Havana anti-Castro underground!

"When you do use local people, often as not you don't handle them properly. Oddly enough, Americans don't know how to use money in intelligence work. For instance, I spend $50.00 a month on a government official or an embassy clerk and I am assured of steady information. You people offer, say $250.00, and here is what happens:

"Your new informant gets excited. He is suddenly impressed by what he has to sell. He gets greedy. He makes up wild reports which he thinks you want to hear. After a while, he starts thinking about further exploiting his position.

"So he comes to me and I give him $50.00 merely to see what he is giving you. Sooner or later, he is going to go to the opposition—the Commies—and make the same offer. They buy. Then from time to time they or I feed your agent a bit of information to see what will get him excited. Sometimes, a very interesting situation can develop that way!

"No," the colonel sighed unhappily, "your people are too nice for this business. Somebody looks you straight in the face and tells you what you want to hear and you believe him. He tells you what you want to hear—and what Castro or Khrushchev wants you to hear—and you believe him. You believe in people. Me, long ago I learned not to trust anybody. I don't have your faith in people, but neither do I get so many of them killed."

The colonel had the facts going for him. One of his points cannot be stressed enough: political warfare in the Caribbean and other less civilized areas is an endless series of truly epic deceptions, duplicity and betrayals, and the Western mentality shrinks from accepting that reality. Of course, nothing is more logical than to attempt to infiltrate your opposition and manipulate it against itself. It should be equally obvious that if the stakes of claw and fang are too high, you shouldn't play the game. The trouble with North Americans is that they try to compromise between virtuous principle and ruthless necessity. That, as the colonel complained, kills people.

Another truism was brought home to me once when I was questioned by U.S. agents regarding a Caribbean intelligence service with which I was associated. I was solemnly asked whether the agents could be identified by a hidden tatoo, carried secret ID cards or used secret handshakes. I answered that this highly efficient service had no need of such exotic practices, that it was hopelessly primitive by their standards, that most of the "agents" were amateur help who earned, maybe, two hundred dollars a month at the most. They refused to believe it. My point is this:

What is not understood by U.S. officials is that in these explosive countries—Latin America, Asia, the Middle East —vitually every man above the age of six is a potential or practicing conspirator, espionage agent, terrorist, guerilla, propagandist and so forth. It is these people who make and break governments and they are constantly reshaping the world.

This massive semi-official or unofficial subversion confronts Western intelligence and diplomatic services with a baffling situation: Their services are geared for action against enemy states and trained enemy spies. These services get to know each other pretty well, they know how their enemies operate, and they know what action can be expected to bring which pattern of response.

But the swarm of amateurs are unknown quantities. The very fact that they are untrained in the conventional techniques makes them more dangerous. The amateur help is also difficult to identify, and is more fanatical and vicious than most professionals.

This situation would probably exist, cold war or no cold war. The only question is how to adapt to it, how to *use* all these free enterprising subversives. For all their monolithic organization, the Reds do an excellent job of adjusting themselves to the freelancers and utilizing their boundless energy. The Reds take over these agents by default because U.S. intelligence regards the amateurs as "unreliable."

The remarks of a tough Cuban exile prompted me to write this chapter. Shortly after the Cuban invasion fiasco, he said to me, "Did the U.S. Government really expect to get rid of Castro with those yacht club boys?"

The remark was unfair. However, this man knows, as I know, how the game is played in our part of the world. It is tough, ruthless, with no quarter given or asked for. I know what I'm talking about. For 15 years I was an officer in Trujillo's intelligence service. I began as field agent and rose to the rank of Chief of Intelligence.

As a young captain two years out of West Point, I was recruited into the Intelligence Service in 1945. In those days, there was no Dominican Intelligence Service as such. In addition to regular duties, officers were temporarily assigned to that job in headquarters.

It was only in later years, through my efforts and those of my successor, that the Intelligence Service became organized and shaped along somewhat conventional, governmental lines. It became centralized. As chief, I was no longer permitted to do field work, but I tried to give my boys every facility. Later, I realized that by doing so I had actually impaired their efficiency. On a far vaster scale, the Bay of Pigs episode revealed that U.S. intelligence suffers from the same defect.

The lesson I learned was this: intelligence work is so

specialized that the quality suffers when any prescribed or standard procedure is followed. Intelligence work simply cannot be stereotyped. There is no room in intelligence for the organization man, or the committee. Yet, inevitably, the problems created by bureaucracy and bureaucrats are going to creep into any organized system.

The evolution of the Central Intelligence Agency is a case in point. When the CIA occupied its immense, new quarters, with its splendid organization, almost unlimited expenses and so on, the tendency seemed to be toward committee work on "political trends," "social developments," "evaluations" and "re-evaluations" (not to mention the monster pastime of them all: "coordination").

And in the maze of reports, memos, recommendations, levels of coordination—the individual agent—the one who is supposed to do the work—got lost in the shuffle. And so did his reports. That is why today's "intelligence reports" are so often in yesterday's newspapers.

But let's go back to the Dominican Intelligence Service. At the beginning, there were about a half dozen agents who covered Mexico, Venezuela, Colombia—all Central America. Each agent had a carefully developed network of contacts in each country.

One of the best sources of information was (and still is) the brothel. The plump, middle-aged madames invariably have as much inside information as the police chief, and they are willing to gossip about it over a friendly glass of beer. Contact could also be made with certain "underpaid" public officials. In every government there are officials eager to supplement their meager salaries.

In this manner, working on a shoestring budget, a Dominican agent fulfilled his mission, which was, simply stated: to know everything that goes on in the area to which he is assigned and to influence the course of events to the best interests of his country. It was rough duty and casualties were high. Today, of course, the stakes are far higher.

To show you exactly what I am talking about, I have included in the next chapter some of the missions of our Dominican agents, all told in the first person. These over-drinks, post-mission accounts are not for the faint-hearted, but tell in graphic terms what politics in Latin America is like. All of the names and places have been changed; otherwise, the following incidents took place exactly as stated.

11

Trujillo's
Network of Terror

I T WAS my first mission, and came close to being my last.

Victor Durand, a veteran Caribbean agent, was in charge of the operation. I was to go along as his assistant. I was sent mainly to observe an old pro in action, and to get acquainted with our contacts in that particular country.

Our mission was fairly simple. We were to land a cargo of contraband munitions and turn it over to a secret revolutionary group. Needless to say, the government of that country was unfriendly to us.

Actually, the groundwork for the operation had already been laid. Durand had gone in on a previous trip to arrange the exact place, date and hour of the arms delivery. We were to slip into the country in a *balandro,* a small schooner, land the guns, and then Durand would give me a week of on-the-job training.

The trip in the *balandro* was uneventful. We looked like any other island schooner hauling fruit, vegetables and copra. At 2:00 on a moonlit morning we approached the coast and spotted two brief flashes of light, the prearranged signal. We sailed on into a tiny cove.

The ship dropped anchor about fifty yards offshore. A dinghy was lowered and Durand and I rowed to the sandy beach . . . and into the expectant arms of secret police chief Augusto Sebastian!

This Sebastian had quite a reputation. He was a Spaniard and a Communist—a peculiarly deadly combination—who was notorious for the atrocities he committed during the Spanish Civil War. He had fled Spain at the end of the war, had migrated to Latin America, and then clawed his way to his present position. No doubt about it, Sebastian was efficient.

As I say, Sebastian was a cold-blooded Communist, but he was also Spanish and capable of burning hatred. He and Durand had tangled before. There was a violent enmity between them which transcended politics.

Sebastian vented his hatred on Durand by castrating him on the spot and letting him bleed to death. The crew of the *balandro* was machinegunned. As for me, the young novice, "beat him to death," Sebastian told his men.

They did a pretty good job. I was beaten into a bloody, shapeless mass and thrown over a cliff. I was left for dead. Almost dead, yes, but not quite. Members of the opposition underground got word of what had happened. They investigated, found me still breathing on a desolate beach, and hauled me to safety. I was taken to an island off the coast and another *balandro* brought me home.

I spent four months in the hospital. Four months to think about Sebastian. He became an obsession. Released from the hospital, I immediately requested permission to return. The Chief nodded understandingly. He knew well the compulsion bred by personal vendettas.

I was put ashore in exactly the same spot as before, the tiny cove. This time, however, no word was sent in advance, so there was no leak. Disguised as a peasant, I made my way to the capital and tried to get in touch with our contacts there.

The revolutionary movement was demoralized, I found, and oppositionists were afraid to make the slightest move. Amateurs, they had been no match for Sebastian's ruthless professionalism. They refused me when I urged them to help me liquidate Sebastian.

I studied the situation. Sebastian always had a large escort. His headquarters was a bristling fortress. His house was well guarded. But, somehow, I had to get to him.

Despite the guards, Sebastian was most vulnerable at his house. That wasn't saying very much, but it was the only possible place. More specifically, the approach would have to be through Sebastian's kitchen.

I had noticed that the cook, a nondescript Indian woman, went to market every day. I had also noticed that the guards never paid any attention to her, nor to any of the other servants whose quarters were in the back of the house. And Sebastian's servants were sometimes visited by those of neighboring houses.

So I set out to woo the cook. Dressed in my shabby peasant's clothing, I followed her around the market place. Finally I saw an opportunity to make advances. Very quickly, Maria and I were having a passionate affair. As I say, poor Maria was no beauty and eagerly responded to my romancing.

It was only a matter of time before Maria was taking me past the guards and into her room at the rear of the house. I wasn't even questioned. But believe me, the toughest proposition in that particular job was making love to that cook. My God, how she stank!

But everything else was going well. I learned Sebastian's habits. He was rarely alone, I discovered, until about midnight when he went upstairs to bed. That was the opening I needed.

One night I left Maria in an exhausted, blissful sleep and slipped up the stairs to Sebastian's room. At about 1:00 A.M. I heard him enter the house and dismiss his escort. He walked upstairs, opened his bedroom door, and literally never knew what hit him.

By the time he recovered consciousness, Sebastian was

bound, gagged and sitting in a chair facing a full-length mirror. Three strands of primer cord were wound around his head. One strand of that explosive wrapped around a palm tree is enough to cut it down like a power saw. I hoped that Sebastian would know that. By the look in his eyes, I knew he did.

"This is a three-minute time fuse attached to a nonelectric cap," I explained to Sebastian. "You know what primer cord is. When it explodes three minutes from now, your head is going to go through the roof."

Then I lit the fuse.

His eyes had been bulging from his head. Suddenly, however, his lids dropped and his body sagged. I stared at Sebastian for a moment, then shook him. It was no use. I felt his pulse. Nothing. He was dead, dead from fright or a heart attack.

I couldn't afford to linger to admire my handiwork. I raced back downstairs, pulled the master power switch and blacked out the house and grounds. Almost simultaneously, Sebastian exploded. And, as the guards rushed the house, I went over the wall at a place I had previously selected while holding hands with Maria.

Sebastian's demise touched off a wave of repression. Inevitably, the brutal crackdown produced an equal wave of popular hostility against the regime. Finally, the armed forces intervened. The government was overthrown and a military junta took over.

So, in a roundabout way, my mission was accomplished.

Caribbean conspirators are firm believers in the old adage: "If at first you don't succed, try and try again." So, one Central American political group made 13 attempts on the life of Nicaraguan President Anastasio ("Tacho") Somoza. On the 14th try, they scored.

But the organizer of this particular operation—an internationally known politician who manages to be both a State Department favorite and an ally of the Latin American extreme left—became somewhat discouraged after the eighth abortive attempt against "Tacho." He decided to let up on Somoza for a while and have a go at Trujillo. As usual, we promptly got word of the tactical shift. The message was flashed to the Dominican National Palace that the chief conspirator, who was the leading citizen of a Central American republic, had decided to try his luck at knocking off the Generalissimo.

Dominican intelligence reacted with characteristic directness and simplicity. The decision was taken to eliminate that leading citizen before he could eliminate ours.

The Old Man sent for me. I was given the usual sixty-second briefing on the situation and told to leave immediately for Central America. My target would be most vulnerable, I was told, when he visited his mistress. She lived on a rather isolated street in the capital city of that country.

My major problem seemed to be the weapons needed for the job. We had no embassy in that country. That meant that the arms couldn't be brought in by diplomatic pouch. Nor could we afford to lose time by smuggling the guns in through the coast. That would give our target a dangerous head start on his own plans.

Finally, I worked out a scheme. I had a large suitcase reconstructed so that the sides were lined with a disassembled Thompson submachine gun, a Colt .45 pistol, and four hand grenades. I filled the suitcase with clothes for a man of well over six feet, weighing some 250 pounds. This was a security measure. The suitcase would be carried by an agent who was short and slight; he could claim there had been a baggage mix-up if Customs inspectors found the weapons.

Then I took the suitcase to Panama and left it with our ambassador there. The ambassador was instructed to turn it over to the agent who was to deliver it to me. I went on to the capital city of our target's country. I would survey the situation while I waited for my assistant and the suitcase.

This agent was Jorge Malena, alias El Cura (the Priest). Until he was murdered in Cuba a short while later—stabbed 16 times—El Cura was one of the rising stars of Dominican Intelligence. El Cura had earned his alias by having studied four years for the priesthood. He was the ideal intelligence operative: resourceful, courageous, and cool as a block of ice. He could impersonate a priest to perfection and it was his favorite guise.

El Cura was going to need his talents, I discovered. I landed at the airport of the target capital and was jolted by the thorough, systematic customs inspection. Our suitcase could pass the usual haphazard inspection, but not this kind of search. I called our ambassador in Panama to warn El Cura not to come. Too late. He was en route.

I went to the airport to see what would happen. Maybe, somehow, I could help.

The saintly, robed figure next to the last man out of the plane was my dear El Cura. Maybe he could get away with claiming that the clothes in the suitcase were never intended for his slight frame. Maybe, but it was a thin hope at best.

I didn't have to signal El Cura to let him know what he was facing. He recognized it immediately. I also noticed that he looked very pale and was perspiring. That was not at all like El Cura, even under the present circumstances. As I say, he was a very cool operator.

Finally, it was his turn to open his suitcase. I tensed. So did El Cura—and vomited all over the Customs inspector and the suitcase. "Air sick," he mumbled, "air sick."

Well, two disgusted Customs men literally carried our agent and his bag, barely opened, to a taxi. Reeking with vomit, El Cura feebly blessed them. He told me later that he had swallowed an emetic just before leaving the plane. He was taking no chances.

We now got down to business. It turned out that the information received at the Palace was only partly correct. Sure enough, the "leading citizen" was plotting to kill Trujillo. And our target did have a mistress at the address indicated. *But*, he didn't visit her. He had her taken periodically to his ranch outside of town. I know from experience that the ranch was virtually impregnable.

We realized that it would be impossible to assassinate our man with our present limited resources. But we could do the next best thing. We could go after the henchmen directly involved in the plot to kill the Chief.

I bought a jeep. (It gives you a better in-and-out mobility than a car.) I drove, the Colt and two hand grenades under my jacket. El Cura, minus his robes, had the other two hand grenades and the submachine gun, covered with a canvas, at his feet on the floor of the jeep. When he had to carry the gun, El Cura merely wrapped it in canvas and held it like a bag of groceries.

We watched the traffic between our man's ranch and the city. We followed the girl's car when she was brought back from her trips to the ranch. We noted that the ranch visitors converged on a noisy little bar on the outskirts of the city. After a few more days of observation, we got the picture.

Our plan was simple in concept and execution. We set fire to a warehouse a block or two away. Then we strolled into the bar. The patrons and the policeman on duty soon noticed the blaze and rushed to the warehouse. The henchmen remained in a private, back room. We lobbed two grenades through the transom and walked back out of the place. And that was that.

The leading citizen got the message. He went back to the business of assassinating Somoza.

We disassembled our still-virgin submachine gun, carefully oiled and wrapped in canvas. We buried it under a tree by a little country road outside the capital. . . . It might be useful some time, you know. I suppose it's still there. (If you ever need a submachine gun in that country, just let me know.)

The Chief called me into his office and explained the situation:

Some American officials were diverting a 12-truck convoy of munitions from Korea, at the beginning of the Korean War, to a point south of the Rio Grande. The munitions were to be sold as "agricultural equipment" to a motley international army known as the Caribbean Legion.

The Legion was formed to topple right-wing dictatorships in the Caribbean. The year before, in fact, the Legion had made an airborne invasion of the Dominican Republic. The invasion had been a dismal and bloody failure. (Some of the invaders who escaped to nearby Haiti ended up in Haitian stew pots.) Nevertheless, there was a real possibility that another attempt would be made.

Trujillo got his information from a member of the Legion command. It seems that this fellow had found revolutionairing to be not much of a paying proposition, and he knew that Trujillo always came across in cash for valuable intelligence.

My job was to check the veracity of the reports, Trujillo told me, and to take whatever action the situation required. The Caribbean Legion was not to get those arms.

I made contact with the convoy at a sleepy, incredibly hot little port on the Gulf of Mexico. As luck would have it, the convoy had arrived one day ahead of the Legion representative who was to take delivery. That gave me a whole day to operate unhindered.

In charge of the convoy was a tall, handsome, crewcut German. I eyed him for a while as he paced the dock on which his trucks were parked. I decided to play it by ear. I walked over:

"Move your trucks to the other wharf," I said to him,

hoping his response would give me a clue on how to handle him.

"Oh, you must be Ramos," Crewcut answered. "Where the hell have you been?" Ramos was the Legion agent he was to have met.

"I was delayed. Come on, let's go have a beer and talk this over."

Crewcut liked beer. I hope he enjoyed those beers that afternoon and evening. They were his last.

Early next morning there was a knock at the door of my hotel room. It was Ramos, just as I was planning to take over the convoy and complete what would have been the biggest coup of my career!

"Where is the German?" Ramos asked sweetly. "I've been looking for him. They tell me he was out drinking beer with you last night."

Now José Angel Ramos and I had a sort of grudging admiration for each other. This was not the first time we had clashed. Once we had spent 14 hours and five bottles of cleren (Haitian firewater) unsuccessfully trying to convince each other to switch sides. Our relations were such that we went to the men's room together so neither of us would have a chance to tamper with the drinks.

So here was José Angel, dangerous as a rattlesnake and just as welcome. I had to try to get him off my back.

"José Angel, my friend, what are you talking about? What German?"

"You know what German. I arrived here late last night. I can't find the German but I do find you. I also hear that you were seen with him. And I hear that you have been acting like you own the convoy."

"José Angel, I can prove that I spent the night with The most lovely girl on the waterfront. Her name is Rosita. I'll introduce you to her. You'll like Rosita."

That was mainly true. I had spent part of the night with Rosita. And she was lovely.

Ramos didn't bother to answer.

"You're slipping, my friend," he said. "Not only were you seen with the German in the cantinas, you were also spotted leading him to a rowboat. You put something in his drink. Where did you dump the body?"

"That's not true," I answered heatedly. "In this warm water he would bloat and come to the surface in a few hours. You know that."

"Yes, and I also know that you know that a corpse doesn't surface if the belly is slit." José Angel was very cynical.

The discussion might have ended in bloodshed if the police hadn't suddenly appeared. They arrested me in connection with the strange disappearance of Crewcut. I had been seen drinking with him, they charged, and later had been seen taking him to a rowboat.

I knew damned well that no one had seen me take Crewcut out in the bay. José Angel had simply figured how he himself would have handled matters. Then he had bribed a couple of fishermen to swear they had seen me. As I say, Ramos and I knew each other quite well.

An idea came to me as I paced up and down in that hot, stinking cell. I bribed a guard to send for Rosita. She came immediately. I sketched out my plan and she got the picture the first time around. Rosita, besides being extremely intelligent, also liked a fast peso as well as anybody. She agreed to help.

The plan was simple. She was to go to the hospital and get a corpse. She was to put it in a casket and have it hauled to her apartment. Then she would report to the police that Crewcut had died there the night before and was ready to be buried. Transparent, yes, but all this would be accompanied, of course, by a generous distribution of a large sum of money the Chief had allocated for the mission. The local authorities didn't mind too much if we foreigners cut each other's throats, but a façade had to be manufactured to take them off the hook.

"Please keep expenses down," were my last words to Rosita. In this business, cash is about the only form of life insurance.

Rosita was back in less than two hours. A doctor at the hospital was willing to cooperate. He would also sign a death certificate giving heart attack as cause of death. And the doctor was the mayor's cousin and a close friend of the police chief.

There was only one problem. The only available corpse was that of a skinny, little, old Indian. It weighed about 90 pounds. Crewcut had weighed about 210.

"When did the Indian die?" I asked.

"Yesterday afternoon."

"Fine," I told her, "he'll do. Put a couple sacks of sand or something in the casket. In this heat, the stench will already be such that no one will want to get near the casket, let alone open it."

It worked.

The German Vice-Consul at the large city 60 miles away came for the funeral. So did Rosita, who wept and beat her breast—where she had stuffed the bills she had made on the deal. A number of the local citizenry were heard to comment that only a gringo would die while enjoying Rosita.

I had already been released and I also attended the funeral. And José Angel also turned up. He knew what had happened, of course, but he knew better than to get involved in a fight with city hall. There would be other days.

But the convoy remained. The trucks had been placed under police guard while I was in jail—Crewcut had signed the consignment of "agricultural equipment" over to me just before he passed away—and Ramos had spent all his money in paying off the Americans who had originally diverted the convoy. He had no funds left for bribes. But by now Ramos did have his people in the area to take delivery.

José Angel and his men would clobber me as soon as I left the city limits. I was an impasse.

"Let's go have a drink and talk this over," I suggested.

"An excellent idea," he said, "but no beer, eh?"

These stories are all typical of Caribbean politics. Trujillo plotted endlessly against enemies; his enemies plotted endlessly against him (and others are now conspiring against his successor.) Latin American "reactionaries" like Trujillo and Somoza shared a common failing with "liberals" such as Venezuela's Romulo Betancourt and Costa Rica's Pepe Figueres: they couldn't keep their claws to themselves. We in the Caribbean have a compulsion to reform, liberate or assassinate our neighbors. (However, on thinking it over, I realize that that compulsion is not confined to the Caribbean.)

Trujillo occasionally went a bit haywire in his own efforts to enlighten the Western Hemisphere. He never turned down an opportunity to help bring friends to power or unseat enemies. This involved him in some mighty weird propositions. For instance, he once told me to turn over 50 submachineguns to an Argentine who claimed to have been sent by Juan Peron. The guns were to overthrow the then-government of Argentina and restore Peron to power.

Shaken by the fact that the Argentine seemed to have convinced the Old Man he could take over Argentina with 50 machineguns, I pleaded for a delay. I wanted to check with Peron, then in exile in Venezuela. Peron, who is quite lucid, promptly disavowed his "envoy" as some kind of a nut.

As a rule, however, Trujillo tended to be cautious. His general policy was to avoid rocking the boat. He had wealth and power. These he sought to protect by secret alliances with other strongman governments. Generally, however, this was a one-way proposition. Nicaragua was an example.

One night in October, 1956, I received a frantic call from the Nicaraguan Consul General in New York, Chato Lang. I was then serving as Dominican Consul General in that city. Chato told me that he had gotten a telephone call from "Tachito," Gen. Anastasio Şomoza, Jr., chief of the Niaraguan Army and a personal friend of mine in Nicaragua. His father, strongman Tacho Somoza, had been shot and was not expected to live. Tachito hadn't been able to get a call through to the Dominican Republic. He had told Lang to contact me so that I could inform Trujillo.

Tacho Somoza had been Trujillo's anchor man in Central America. I knew he would respond to a plea for help from the Nicaraguan government. I put the call through to Trujillo. His reaction was what I had expected: I was to tell the Somoza brothers (the other brother was Luis, President of the Nicaraguan Congress and next in line for the presidency) not to worry. He, Trujillo, would throw his weight behind them. And he did.

The Old Man immediately sent word to Central America. Anybody who tried to buck the Somoza boys would have to deal with him. He made his point even clearer: a contingent of picked Dominican troops was airlifted to Nicaragua. Ostensibly, the troops were to be an honor guard at Tacho's funeral. But they also took combat gear and live ammo.

Trujillo's decisive move saved the day for the Somozas. Luis was sworn in as president and settled down to running the country. A few months later, the Old Man sent me over to Nicaragua to look things over and strengthen the alliance. Both brothers swore undying gratitude for Trujillo's aid. Another Trujillo agent, an American who had once worked for the late Tacho, was permitted to make duplicates of intelligence reports in Tacho's files.

But that was about the extent of the Nicaraguans' reciprocation. Four years later, when Trujillo's star was dimming and the Somoza brothers had been accepted in the inter-American community, Nicaragua readily voted to condemn Trujillo at the Costa Rica conference of the Organization of American States.

A practical man, Trujillo merely shrugged. "Well, what do you expect," he said. "They don't need me now." That was true. Trujillo had outlived his day and his usefulness to his neighbors.

12

"Accident-Suicide-Heart Attack"

"**O**UR Dominican agents would have gotten lost in the New York subways," I once told an American official who asked about the celebrated disappearance of Columbia University professor Jesus Galindez. I also told him that this worked two ways, that U.S. agents are equally ill-equipped to cope with the political jungles of the Caribbean. To me, the most vivid example of this fact is not Cuba, it is Guatemala: specifically, the assassination of Carlos Castillo Armas, President of Guatemala.

At about 9 P.M. on July 26th, 1957, President Armas left his private chambers in the National Palace at Guatemala City and entered a darkened hall. Four shots rang out. The President died instantly.

His death was the culmination of a conspiracy already known to diplomats and intelligence officials in capitals from Washington to Rio de Janeiro. It was also the culmination of a career of the man who led the only successful anti-Communist liberation movement in history. In June, 1954, aided by the CIA, Castillo Armas' patriots smashed the Communist government of President Jacabo Arbenz. Guatemala ceased to be the first Communist stronghold in this hemisphere.

Ironically, the Castillo Armas assassination was a factor in Trujillo's own death four years later. A former Dominican race track tout, Johnny Abbes Garcia, demonstrated great skill and accuracy in reporting to Trujillo the developing Guatemalan conspiracy. Impressed by the prophecy, Trujillo made Johnny a lieutenant-colonel and placed him in charge of Dominican security forces. Anybody who could penetrate a foreign assassination plot so thoroughly would surely be even more reliable on his home grounds.

But Trujillo was mistaken. Johnny's subsequent repressive tactics alienated Trujillo from his people, from the world, and from the specific officers and politicians who finally murdered him. Trujillo was slain in a conspiracy remarkably similar to that which killed the Guatemalan president.

Trujillo's interest in Castillo Armas and Guatemala went far back, back to the years 1949-54 during which a state of semi-war prevailed between our two nations. Trujillo feared and hated Guatemala's Communist regime and encouraged the anti-Communist revolutionary movement. When Castillo Armas triumphed, Trujillo regarded him as a friend and ally. The intelligence services of both governments became tightly interwoven.

In fact, by 1956 whole segments of the Guatemalan secret service were controlled more by Trujillo than by Armas. Not only was there working cooperation between the two services; Trujillo also put scores of Guatemalan agents on his payroll. Eventually, Trujillo, through Johnny Abbes, knew more about what was happening in Guatemala that did Armas.

I learned, for instance, that as early as January, 1957, a major conspiracy to overthrow Castillo Armas was shaping up in official Guatemalan circles. We were not particularly surprised to note that the plotters included both high ranking military men and ardent leftists. Such alliances are not uncommon in the Caribbean.

Neither were we surprised when a clandestine radio went on the air in March, 1957, announced as La Voz Dominicana, Trujillo's own powerful Dominican station. The transmitters carried diatribes against Castillo Armas and threats of assassination—all in the name of La Voz Dominicano and Trujillo.

Confusion tactics such as the above are standard operating procedure in a Caribbean conspiracy. Until his death, virtually every political upheaval south of the Florida straits would be attributed to Trujillo. And Trujillo secretly delighted in that fact. Once, in 1958, an Argentine newspaper reported a crop failure in some province, commenting that "some sectors of public opinion are convinced that Trujillo caused this situation." The Chief was immensely pleased by the tribute.

But Trujillo was curiously impotent in his efforts to save Castillo Armas. On May 22nd, a Guatemalan secret agent, Ruben Arriloa Gomez, warned his President that his closest associates were plotting his death. Castillo Armas shrugged off the report.

That was a typical Armas reaction to bad news. He was a strange person, dreamy, almost mystical. At times, he lived in another world. But while Castillo Armas floated in the clouds, conspiracy and corruption flourished on Guatemala's newly liberated soil. Both the regular army, which hated Castillo's "Liberation Army," and the Communists conspired to destroy their common "enemy."

On May 25, our agents reported a secret meeting at a house at 14-04 Avenida Reforma in Guatemala City. Present was Felipa Mendoza, a plump, middle-aged lady who was a crack agent for Castillo Armas' personal intelligence staff. Outside the house our agents noted the license plate numbers of the guests. I still have the list, one of the many documents I carried into my Canadian exile. They were P 6009, P 6992, O 240, O 164, P 4-470, P 1766, P 20-883, O 435, O 48.

Most important was the license plate 12-239. It belonged to none other than the chief of Castillo's general staff, Col. José Magdaleno Ortega. The conspirators included (Felipa Mendoza reported) the chief of police, two members of the

Presidential general staff, plus an assortment of other top government officials. Also present were several known Communists or pro-Communists.

Felipa Mendoza drew up a complete report of the secret meeting and presented it to her superior, Carlos Lemus, Sub-Chief of Security. Nothing happened. Suddenly, Felipa realized what was happening. Security reports were routed to the President through staff chief Colonel Ortega. And Ortega and his Palace conspirators effected an iron curtain of silence around the President. He was being sealed off from the outside world.

It was then that we went into action in a desperate effort to save Castillo. The Guatemalan ambassador in the Dominican Republic was notified. Agents in Guatemala City called on the U.S. Embassy in an effort to use the power of the United States to break through the wall of isolation thrown about the president. In Ciudad Trujillo, an American on Trujillo's staff carefully outlined the conspiracy to the American Embassy's capable young political officer. Trujillo even ordered that warnings be beamed to Guatemala over La Voz Dominicana.

In Guatemala, meanwhile, Felipa continued to fight for her President's life. She was blocked at every turn. She wrote a series of letters to the President. They never reached him. She contacted the Minister of Defense and described the situation. His reply was that Col. Ortega was responsible only to the President and that any information should be dispatched through the proper channels. He took no other action—other than to report the incident to Col. Ortega. Ortega then saw to it that Felipa was ousted from the service.

By this time, even the bootblacks of Guatemala knew pretty much what was happening. Only Castillo Armas remained serenely ignorant of his approaching execution. Yet, perhaps he was not entirely unaware of what was happening.

A few days before his death, Castillo Armas told Brazilian Ambassador Francisco D'Almo Lousada that his life was in danger and that that might be the last time they would meet. Beyond this, however, the Guatemalan President gave no indication that he was aware of the by then massive conspiracy against him. A strange man, Castillo Armas.

"Castillo Armas will be executed," Johnny Abbes reported to Trujillo, "between July 24 and August 2." That came in the middle of July. Each morning, Trujillo would call Johnny to his office for a report. On July 24th, Abbes pinpointed the execution: "President Castillo Armas will die the day after tomorrow."

And he did.

Immediately thereafter, there was a flurry of activity while the Guatemalans went through the motions of investigating the murder. U.S. experts with lie detectors were rushed in. To no one's surprise, it was learned that officers and men of the President's own guard had participated in the plot. Then the government began to investigate everyone but the actual assassins. And, as expected, there was a barrage of charges that Trujillo was behind it all.

The Castillo Armas case has long fascinated Caribbean intelligence circles. The U.S. State Department and CIA were informed well in advance what was happening. The U.S. government was the only power really capable of breaking through the isolation imposed on the Guatemalan president by his staff. And the U.S. had a huge investment, in money and prestige, in Castillo Armas. Yet, it did nothing.

That case offers a striking contrast with another incident which took place about the same time. Trujillo's American aide had contacted the U.S. Embassy's political officer, Bob Allen, and warned him that from his reports from Guatemala, Cuba and Haiti, there was a plan afoot by the Cuban rebels to kidnap Earl T. Smith, U.S. Ambassador to Cuba.

The aide emphasized to Allen that the report was unconfirmed. However, in view of the fact that it came from several sources, he felt that the State Department should be alerted, "just in case."

There was an instantaneous reaction. Smith was immediately put under constant guard and U.S. Marines were even posted in his bedroom.

The contrast between Washington's reaction to the two different warnings was startling, arousing a great deal of speculation that the State Department wanted Castillo Armas out of the way. I don't think that's the answer.

I believe that routine, bureaucratic sluggishness in the American service was the important factor. Once the Communists were routed from Guatemala in 1954, the topnotch people assigned there were replaced by men of lesser experience. Guatemala had dropped out of the headlines, and Washington is responsive more to headlines than anything else.

So it was not surprising that Roy Rubottom, then the State Department's top Latin American affairs officer, should turn up in Guatemala City just before the assassination and announce that he was delighted that things were going so well for Guatemala.

Little by little, this sort of thing has come into public view, revealing that Washington suffers from what is now called an "intelligence gap." To Trujillo, the "gap" seemed more like a bottomless canyon, but he never stopped trying. In 1948, he warned that the Communists were planning to launch what became known as the *Bogotozo*. Those were bloody riots in the capital of Colombia, riots which almost broke up the Pan American conference being held there, and which sparked a bloody civil war which has cost some 300,000 lives and is still being waged.

And we also warned Washington about Fidel Castro, supplying a thick dossier covering his career all the way back to the 1948 Bogotoza and before. Our warnings were, obviously, to no avail. (Even Trujillo himself, as I will show in a later chapter, played a major role in helping Castro to power. Both Trujillo and Castro later wanted to forget that fact.)

Dominican intelligence warned of the 1949 Communist infiltration, and subsequent take-over of Guatemala. The warnings were ignored until almost too late. Our agents reported plans to attack the then Vice-President Richard Nixon when he visited Caracas in 1958. "Is that so?" commented the U.S. intelligence official to whom we gave the reports. "We have heard similar warnings from other sources." But nothing was done, and Nixon was almost lynched.

A few weeks after the Nixon fracas, we turned over another tip to the United States. President Eisenhower's brother Milton had planned a trip to Central America. Then he cancelled it following Nixon's treatment. Then the State Department announced that the trip would be made after all, but that Milton would be "virtually invisible."

"All the elaborate security is not necessary, " we told our same intelligence official. "Milton will be safe enough. No hostile actions are being planned."

"Is that so?" said the agent. "That's the same word we get from other sources."

But Milton scurried about Central America like a frightened fugitive from justice. He used curtained limousines which raced along back roads. His itinerary was a guarded secret. Everything was so super-secret that some of Milton's own entourage got lost along the way. The Central Americans laughed at the spectacle. What Milton's reaction was I don't know.

The most important factor in our calculating of Caribbean political trends was this: almost every developing political upheaval in the middle Americas gives advance tremors in Mexico City. (Nearly all of the episodes just recounted came from our Mexican sources.) The progress of the plot to assassinate Guatemalan President Armas was partially gauged by tapping sources of information in Mexico City. The January, 1960, bomb conspiracy in the Dominican Republic was tipped off in Mexico City during October, 1959.

The fact that Mexico is the Caribbean's most sensitive political seismograph makes the city an espionage center, a listening post both indispensable and dangerous.

Foreign agents are accident-prone in the Mexican capital: "traffic accidents," "heart attacks" and "suicides" have taken a heavy toll. All three forms of meeting death can easily disguise murder, and properly worded death certificates are ridiculously easy to come by.

Automoble "accidents" came into prominence in the early 1950's. Those were the years when an extraordinary number of Guatemalan anti-Communist exiles were mowed down by Mexico City vehicles.

Since then, no one involved in the 1954 liberation of Guatemala can have a normal, non-political car wreck. When John Peurifoy, U.S. Ambassador to Guatemala who played a major role in that episode, was reported killed in a car crash in Thailand, people all over the Caribbean nodded knowingly. It was to be expected, they said.

I don't know about Thailand, but I do know that many Caribbean conspirators of different nationalities have picked up the accident-suicide-heart attack habit in Mexico City and developed it into an art.

The Mexican secret police view all this with a sort of detachment. They have a philosophy that is very precise: you can get away with murder if the cops can be convinced that the victim was "against Mexico." You can engage in all sorts of frenetic agitation and violence as long as these activities are aimed at any government other than that of Mexico. The police will make available their secrets and services, if they are sure they will not be used against the best interests of Mexico.

It may surprise you to learn that the Mexican federal

cops are second to none in the cloak-and-dagger industry. They are real professionals. They possess all the modern skills and training, plus an instinctive flair for intrigue.

That is why the services of Mexican detectives are used by just about every intelligence group in the Caribbean. It's a unique set-up. For a fee, the Guatemalan government can expect to get a detailed, accurate report on Guatemalan exile activities in Mexico. The same police might also look the other way while arms are being smuggled across the Mexican border to rebel guerrillas in Guatemala—however they would also make sure that the same amount of arms left Mexico as entered.

It is in this atmosphere that Caribbean conspirators wage their secret wars. Sometimes it is rough on the by-standers. An example of this sorry fact occurred in the 1950's, when I was sent to Mexico on a mission. The opposition spotted me and several attempts were made on my life. These ceased when the hotel where I was staying was bombed. I wasn't even scratched. The opposition had blown up another hotel room and its occupant, one Rafael Rodriguez, who unfortunately bore the very same name I was using as my "cover."

On another occasion, a zealous Trujillo agent learned that a Guatemalan Communist named José Perez was in-volved in a conspiracy against the Old Man. Investigating further, the agent found that there were no less than *three* José Perez's in the Guatemalan Communist Party. Which one was the guilty party? Who to kill? He solved his prob-lem in a drastic manner: there is now not a single José Perez left in the Guatemalan Communist party. This seem-ingly insignificant incident can be said to be the story of Caribbean conspiracy. Repeated in a countless variety of ways, often on a far vaster scale, this incident holds the essence of the jungle politics of Latin America.

13

Displaced Dictators–
The Ominous Prelude

TRUJILLO's own fall seemed far in the future in the late 1950's. But during the same year as Castillo Armas' assassination, the first of an influx of displaced dictators sought sanctuary in the Old Man's seemingly impregnable stronghold. First to arrive was Rojas Pinilla of Venezuela, then came Perez Jimenez of Venezuela, followed by Argentina's Peron, and finally, Batista of Cuba.

I could never understand why Trujillo admitted this parade of broken strongmen. Among other things, their presence drew attention to his own iron-fisted dictatorship. And, except for Peron, he held them all in active contempt. But my instructions were explicit: they were to be treated as honored guests (although, in some instances, as paying guests).

First to arrive was Rojas Pinilla in 1957. As top ranking officer of the Colombian armed forces, he had come to power by pledging to end the bloody civil war between Colombian Liberals and Conservatives. He was partly successful. For a year or two, Rojas Pinilla was a national hero. Then, inevitably, the honeymoon came to an end. His ham-handed tactics were resented by the leaders of both parties, the oligarchy—as he called the Colombian upper class; the Colombian social structure is one of the most feudal in the world—and the middle class. They patched up their feuds, temporarily, and united to overthrow Rojas Pinilla. A bloody turbulence swept the country.

The president and his top military men put their heads together. They decided that Rojas Pinilla should set up a military junta, turn the government over to the junta, and leave the country until the political heat was off. Then he would come back and the junta would transfer its power back to him.

Rojas Pinilla carefully handpicked the officers who would form the junta; all were men on whom he had lavished power and promotions. A shrewd and careful man, Rojas Pinilla.

The plan didn't work, of course. As soon as he was out of the country, Rojas Pinilla's old buddies promptly notified him that the arrangement was for keeps.

That was the sad tale the ex-dictator related to Trujillo. It made a big impression on the Old Man. Those double-crossing Colombian officers had sinned against the entire Latin American dictator fraternity! Trujillo told Rojas Pinilla that he would be delighted to help restore him to power.

This would have been an interesting project, since Colombia is many times bigger than the Dominican Republic. However, a fact came to light which shattered Trujillo's faith in his Colombian guest: Rojas Pinilla was broke. The man who had for years been dictator of a large and wealthy country was almost penniless. To Trujillo, that meant the man was some kind of political nut. It was also a sort of infringement on the rules of the Latin dictator tradition.

But Trujillo went through the motions of honoring the alliance. He let Rojas Pinilla have pocket money by buying the latter's home in Bogota for use as an embassy. The Old Man told me to keep an eye on developments and to help to a limited extent. He himself had lost interest. Even so, Rojas Pinilla did succeed in lining up some top-ranking officers to back him against the junta. We were on the point of flying him back into Colombia when he changed his mind. He felt that the situation was not quite ripe.

The truth is, once they leave they can never make a comeback.

I remember Trujillo's comment when it fizzled out and Rojas Pinilla left Santo Domingo: "Poor man." He meant that in more ways than one. If you want to play power politics in our league, you must have money or you can't play.

Rojas Pinilla didn't have a cent. But our next displaced dictator, Perez Jimenez of Venezuela, was the richest ex-dictator in the club. We knew Perez Jimenez was about finished when our agents sent this report: Venezuelan army officers are saluting with the thumb held down. To the initiate, this meant that "Tom Thumb has to go," referring to the short, plump Jimenez.

The first to voice open criticism of P.J.—as Perez Jimenez was usually called—was his joint chief of staff. P.J. promptly put the general on a plane and sent him to Trujillo for safekeeping. But that was the beginning of the end. Soon P.J. himself was aboard a plane bound for safety in the Dominican Republic.

Trujillo despised P.J. for not putting up much of a fight: he had set a bad example. P.J.'s defense was that he couldn't stand bloodshed. That answer merely irritated Trujillo all the more, of course. How in hell can you be a proper dictator, Trujillo wondered, and not be prepared to shoot people? The answer was that P.J. left all such nasty details to his security chief, Pedro Estrada. Estrada's relationship to P.J. was perhaps summed up in a then-current Venezuelan joke:

P.J. and an earlier Venezuelan dictator, Vicente Gomez, were in hell. Gomez was in manure up to his neck as punishment for his sins. But P.J. was only ankle-deep in excrement.

"How come?" a visitor asked. "After all, P.J. was about as bad as Gomez."

"True," the satanical guide answered, "but P.J. is standing on Pedro Estrada's shoulders."

Actually, Estrada stopped holding up P.J. the day both men fled for the Dominican Republic. Estrada was very bitter at P.J. for quitting. Greed, according to Estrada, was the reason for P.J.'s downfall. Worse, Estrada hadn't received a fair share of the take.

Estrada was bemoaning his poverty to me one day over drinks in the Hotel Embajador cocktail lounge. P.J. had made off with millions and millions, Estrada said with a sob in his voice. And do you think he would share that wealth with his old comrade Pedro? No. He, Pedro Estrada, was doomed to a life of penury.

"That's too bad," I said sympathetically, "but surely you must have salvaged something. Didn't you manage to leave with at least a little money?"

"Well, yes," Estrada answered mournfully, "but only ten million dollars."

Not surprisingly, Trujillo decided that P.J. should pay a little rent for his sanctuary. The relatively modest sum of one million dollars was extracted from him. Even so, P.J. outlived his welcome; he left the Republic, taking with him Trujillo's contempt.

Our next guest was Juan Peron. Of them all, Peron was the only displaced dictator for whom Trujillo had any respect. He was also the most unassuming and friendly. It was common to see him doing his shopping in the local super market. Unlike the others, he never complained or bemoaned his downfall. Peron still remains, of course, one of the most powerful single factors in Argentine politics.

In Trujillo's view, Peron had made two major mistakes: he had quarrelled with the Catholic Church and he had failed to control the armed forces. Trujillo never dreamed that he would one day face a somewhat similar situation.

The last of our displaced dictators was Cuba's Fulgencio Batista. Yet, for years the two dictators had been mortal enemies. Trujillo's fundamental contempt for Batista went far back. Batista had been nothing more than a sergeant when he took power by leading a revolt of non-commissioned officers against their superiors. Trujillo, an officer who had served with the Marines, despised Batista as an uncouth non-com and mutineer.

However, whatever his distaste for Batista personally, the Old Man felt that anti-Communist dictators should stick together. So his was the first government to recognize Batista when the latter ousted Cuban president Carlos Prio in March, 1952. Trujillo subsequently invited Batista to visit the Dominican Republic, and wooed the Cuban strongman in various ways.

The Old Man was coolly snubbed for all his efforts: Batista pointedly ignored Trujillo. The Old Man cursed under his breath, but did nothing.

Matters came to a head when Batista was formally inaugurated as President of Cuba in 1955. I was dispatched to the inauguration ceremony to represent the Dominican Republic. My real mission was to confer with Batista and propose an informal alliance of our two governments. Much as he disliked the one-time Cuban army sergeant, Trujillo considered it prudent to present a united front to the "liberals" in Washington and to revolutionaries in the Caribbean.

I found that Batista was as enthusiastic about an alliance with Trujillo as he would have been to exposure to leprosy. He said he would welcome any secret assistance Trujillo might give him, but for heaven's sake, don't let anyone know about it!

"That sargento de mierda!" Trujillo snarled when I made my report, "I'm going to oust the bastard!" And he proceeded to attempt to do just that. There was immediately launched what was code-named "Operacion Panuelos y Tomates." Panuelos (handkerchiefs) was the code word for arms; Tomates (tomatoes) meant explosives.

Our agents got in touch with one Col. La Rubia of the Cuban army. He was known to be mildly anti-Batista. He was also ardently pro-money. La Rubia was given $100,000 to spend on an attempt to promote an anti-Batista uprising by the Cuban armed forces.

That would be next to impossible, La Rubia reported. The army was loyal to Batista. The most that La Rubia could do would be to neutralize certain key officers and commands, by liberal doses of U.S. dollars.

Trujillo looked around for other allies to war on Batista. At that time, however, the only active anti-Batista elements were led by ousted president Carlos Prio; and Prio was a Trujillo-hater from way back. But that didn't stop the two old enemies from joining forces. That's very common in Caribbean politics.

The yacht *Angelita* was dispatched to Miami. Aboard were Trujillo agents who met with Prio's lieutenants and worked out the terms of the new alliance. It was decided to launch a revolutionary offensive in Cuba's Oriente province, a center of anti-Batista ferment. The Dominican role consisted of smuggling tons of munitions and explosives into Oriente for use by Prio's partisans.

Here is where La Rubia's contacts were needed. He would have to slip a few thousand dollars to key military and naval officers in the provincial command. They would look the other way when the munitions were landed. That could be done in those days, and La Rubia did it.

I made two nerve-wracking trips to Oriente aboard a frigate of the Dominican Navy. I say nerve-wracking not because of danger from the Cuban armed forces. On the contrary, we steamed right up to the coast in broad daylight and discharged our cargo. It was the cargo itself that bothered me. The frigate was a literal powder keg. The decks were practically awash from the weight of tons of dynamite, TNT and other explosives, some of them highly unstable.

Cuban revolutionaries also tend to be somewhat unstable. Despite solemn promises and breast-beating boasts, Prio's rebels failed to move. The munitions, carefully stored in caves and farmhouses, remained untouched.

Disgusted, Trujillo wanted to dispatch a force of Dominican troops to Oriente to spark the revolution. The troops would be disguised as Cubans. The officer who was designated to command these "Cuban guerrillas"? Me. I hastily pointed out that it would be very embarrassing if it became known that a Dominican general and Dominican troops had invaded Cuba. The Old Man reluctantly agreed.

Eventually, however, the munitions were put to use— by Fidel Castro. Prio made a pact with Castro and turned over to him all the weapons and explosives sent by Trujillo. The Chief was outraged. He feared and hated Castro. He knew from my intelligence reports on Fidel that the rebel leader was not just another Caribbean revolutionary. But the end result was that "Operacion Panuelos y Tomates" helped bring to power Trujillo's archenemy. "My dynamite, there goes more of my dynamite," Trujillo would comment sadly each time he read reports of Castro sabotage in Cuba. But there *was* one type of bomb target in Cuba of which the Old Man thoroughly approved: the sugar industry.

The Old Man often mixed sugar in his political brews. It was no coincidence that Panuelos y Tomates was aimed at the largest sugar producing country in Latin America— nor that the Dominican Republic is the second major sugar producer. It was even less of a coincidence that the biggest sugar producer in the Dominican Republic was Trujillo himself.

If Trujillo had managed to smash the Cuban sugar industry—and sent the price of sugar soaring—he would have made millions. Instead, he helped make Fidel Castro.

14

The Castro-Trujillo
Death-Struggle

MY WIFE was shaking me frantically. It was about 5:30 in the morning, January 1, 1959. An hour or two earlier she and I had returned home from a festive and alcoholic reception of the New Year at the Country Club. I was in no shape for phone calls. But one name my wife kept repeating suddenly swept away the mental fog. Trujillo. Trujillo was on the phone. I grabbed the receiver.

"Yes, Chief," I mumbled.

"You remember that report you gave me yesterday regarding the Cuban situation?" Trujillo's voice rasped over the wire. "You told me Batista was strong enough to maintain himself in power for another six months."

"That's right, Chief," I replied.

Actually, that wasn't really true. The Old Man had sent me to Cuba on December 23 and I had returned December 30. I had reported that while the military situation was not bad, the overall situation was hopeless. The Cuban armed forces were hopelessly corrupt, undisciplined and dispirited. However, the rebels were ill-armed and untrained. Batista's army should be able to maintain the status quo for at least a few months more, I had told Trujillo.

"Yes, I know you told me that," Trujillo said in an icy voice. "Now I want you to tell Batista that. He's out at the airport now."

I dressed hastily and raced to the airport. It was true.

Batista and his entourage were assembled in the airport building. All were clean-shaven, wearing immaculate uniforms, and looking as unruffled as if they had arrived on a holiday. They had fled, they said, "to avoid further bloodshed."

In truth, they had beaten themselves. They were not beaten in combat by Fidel's two or three thousand ill-armed, untrained fanatics. Corruption and inefficiency had drained the army of fighting spirit. Cuban army officers had sold whole arsenals to Castro guerrillas. Some garrison commanders had surrendered their entire commands—for a fee. One colonel sold a complete trainload of desperately needed munitions. An army general even supplied Fidel with cigars and brandy while he was supposed to be directing operations against the guerrillas.

It was fitting, I think, that most of those officers didn't get a chance to enjoy their wealth. They were shot—including Colonel La Rubia, our corrupt friend of "Operation Panuelos y Tomates"—or imprisoned. Unfortunately, some of the worst offenders found their way to safety.

And now I had that crowd of military and political hacks on my hands. Trujillo was furious. He was particularly irritated by rumors that he and Batista had secretly arranged in advance that Batista be given asylum in the Dominican Republic. Actually, the first Trujillo knew of it was when Batista's plane requested permission to land.

But that was not important now. Trujillo knew he had a fight on his hands. He had long realized that Castro was unlike any previous Caribbean revolutionary leader. He recognized that Castro was a dedicated fanatic, a man who would never make a binding pact or compromise, since such moves are aimed at fixing a status quo—and Castro was in the world revolution business, serving the Communist notion of destiny.

So Trujillo set out to destroy him. Except for outside intervention, the Old Man might well have succeeded. He was then at the peak of his power, still the most dangerous man in the Caribbean, if not in all Latin America. And Trujillo had been making and breaking Caribbean governments before fuzz had sprouted on Fidel's chin.

But Fidel had powerful protectors in those days. Those guardian angels weren't in Moscow. They were in Washington. Washington officials thwarted Trujillo at every turn during Castro's first few vulnerable months. Those officials tried to prevent arms shipments to anti-Castro Cubans, attacked the leader of the anti-Castro movement, attempted to block undercover operations, and generally just plain fouled up Trujillo's counter-revolution.

There was only one Cuban exile leader, in Trujillo's view, who had the guts and brains to tangle with Fidel: Gen. José Eleuterio Pedraza. Slim, tough Pedraza had risen from private to chief of staff. Over the years he had shown himself to be a dangerous opponent; he was too dangerous, in Batista's opinion, and was purged by him from the army. But when Batista's regime was crumbling, it was to Pedraza that he turned in a final act of desperation. By then it was too late.

Pedraza reached the Dominican Republic shortly after Batista. He conferred with Trujillo. Immediately, a crash program got underway. A "Cuban Liberation Army" was organized and its ranks swelled as hundreds of refugees began to arrive from Florida and Cuba. An exile training camp was set up, former Cuban naval personnel began invasion preparations at our Las Calderas navy base, and exiled air force pilots began service with our own squadrons.

In Cuba, the situation was almost identical. Like Trujillo, Castro knew that it was a struggle to the death between them. Preparations for the invasion of the Dominican Republic had begun within days after Batista's flight. Exiles and revolutionaries from a dozen lands poured into hastily built training camps.

Then, suddenly, there came an astonishing development.

A letter mailed from Miami reached Trujillo. In it, William Morgan, one of Castro's most famous revolutionary heroes, offered to help Pedraza overthrow Fidel. This was the first of a long series of letters from Morgan, an American adventurer, to Trujillo.

Morgan's revolutionary career had begun in February, 1958, when he slipped into Cuba and joined a tiny guerrilla force operating in the Escambray mountains of Las Villas province. Morgan, who had served in the U.S. Army, boasted to the guerrillas of his fabulous exploits as a wartime paratrooper. Actually, he had never seen combat. But the guerrillas accepted him at face value, and soon Morgan was commanding a small but rapidly growing guerrilla force. Despite his lack of experience, Morgan was spectacularly successful.

His troops worshipped him. They fought and won 15 engagements and came to be known as the Tigers of Espesura. Morgan's fame spread, recruits poured in, and his range of operations expanded. By the time Batista fled, Morgan's men dominated perhaps a third of Las Villas province.

We had long been carefully watching the development of the Escambray front. Militarily, it was far more important than the remote mountains of Oriente, Cuba's easternmost province. The Escambray is in the center of the 800-mile-long island and is less than 200 miles from Havana.

Most important, from Trujillo's point of view, was the fact that the Escambray was independent of Castro. Moreover, that independence was obviously a sore point with Fidel. There were intermittent clashes between the Escambray guerrillas and Castro troops which had infiltrated the province.

A pact of sorts between the *fidelistas* and the Escambray had been worked out by Raul Castro. Morgan and his cocommander, Eloy Gutierrez Menoyo, were made majors in the rebel army. Nevertheless, dissension continued. Our own agents fanned suspicion on both sides. We planted the rumor that Morgan wanted to move into Havana and take over before Fidel.

I think we might have succeeded in blowing apart Castro's revolutionary movement if Batista had been able to hold on for a few more months. The Escambray units were just beginning to swell into a powerful force when the government collapsed. But they were still not strong enough to challenge Castro directly. To forestall destruction, Morgan and his men placed themselves under Fidel's orders. Then he contacted us.

In March, 1959, the alliance was cemented. Morgan dispatched an envoy to Ciudad Trujillo. He was Frank Nelson, a middle-aged American businessman who had lived in Havana for 18 years. We had been told that Nelson was coming. He was driven out to Trujillo's San Cristobal ranch for an immediate conference. Pedraza and I were also present.

Frank had an odd but curiously plausible story. He had become involved with Morgan while trying to secure the release of a friend from a Castro prison. The two Americans had become friendly, but it quickly became obvious to Nelson that Castro would never free his friend. And Morgan repeatedly dropped hints that he would need little encouragement to turn against Fidel, letting it be known that he was primarily interested in big chunks of cash. He was available for hire.

Morgan, then, was out to make money; whether it came from Castro, Trujillo, or wealthy Cuban exiles didn't seem to matter.

His first letter to the Chief was dated, I believe, February 24, 1959. Written in English, it was a long, chatty letter, three pages of single-spaced typing. Morgan outlined Fidel's overall plan for the entire Caribbean (very accurately as it now turns out).

He reported the location of various international invasion camps in the Pinar del Rio and Oriente provinces. He described the influx of foreign volunteers from all over the hemisphere and the formation of small exile armies. He predicted the invasions of Panama, Nicaragua, Haiti and the Dominican Republic. He explained the mechanics of the triumvirate—Fidel, Raul and Che Guevara—rule of Cuba. Morgan even predicted his own eventual fall from grace.

His reasons for being willing to betray Castro were explicit: Morgan was a believing Catholic but Castro was consumed by the conviction that Communist revolutionary techniques were a magic formula. Fidel, unlike Raul and Che, was not a Party member, but believed blindly in the power of Communist strategy and tactics. Such tactics had proved effective in the revolution and Castro now considered them invincible in all spheres of action. That, wrote Morgan, was betrayal of the revolution.

And, besides, Morgan hadn't been properly rewarded. He and his men weren't even being paid. The Second Front of the Escambray had also been overlooked when key government posts were passed out. Dissension had set in, and his revolutionists were eager to claim their reward —not to serve some kind of world socialist revolution.

Even from this distance of time, Morgan's letter still seems an extraordinary document. Whatever its intent, his letter was both accurate in its data and in overall analysis. Written in plain, blunt language, the letter bore an overpowering impression of sincerity.

Nevertheless, I had been in this business too long not to be suspicious. Of course, such sudden shifts of allegiance are not uncommon in the Caribbean. Moreover, there were solid facts behind Morgan's hostility to Castro. We knew its roots were from long before Batista's collapse. The danger was, Frank said in summing up his story at the ranch meeting, that Morgan now seemed to be in a position to reap a bonanza on a deal he was negotiating on behalf of the Castro government. It involved the sale of eleven huge Globemaster transport planes to the Cuban government.

Fidel wanted the planes, each capable of carrying 300 men, to use in the subsequent invasion of the Dominican Republic. Morgan would make a commission on the sale and would train the paratroopers to be used in the operation. The government of Venezuelan President Romulo Betancourt was to put up the money for the purchase, Morgan had told Nelson, plus men, guns and pilots.

Nelson had then lied to Morgan, telling him that he had information that Castro was planning to buy the planes from another company and through another intermediary, in the hopes that Morgan would abandon his Globemaster invasion flirtation and concentrate on overthrowing Castro. If the plane deal did materialize, Nelson feared, Morgan's loyalties would shift accordingly.

But the upshot of Nelson's talks with Morgan was that the latter had said the hell with Castro, the Globemaster deal and the invasion of the Dominican Republic. He would help overthrow Castro—for a fee of one million dollars.

The whole thing seemed to me like a damn shaky premise on which to base the overthrow of Castro. But the Old Man merely remarked that it would be a cheap price to pay to get rid of Fidel. He was sold. He agreed to turn over $500,000 to Morgan in two weeks and the other half-million a week before Morgan launched his uprising.

Nelson returned to Havana to present the offer to Morgan. He eagerly accepted. His Second Front organization became the nucleus of an anti-Castro conspiracy.

Another American, my associate in a number of operations, played a key role in Miami. He worked closely with ex-Senator Anselmo Alliegro, one of the few exiles who put up sizeable sums of money for the planned offensive, and representatives of 43 anti-Castro organizations in exile and within Cuba. One of the key figures in the conspiracy was Alexis Hernandez, a young assistant professor of bio-chemistry at the University of Havana.

Plans became more and more elaborate. Al Hernandez was to lead an air attack on Havana. Charges of dynamite were to be dropped, but would explode at a thousand feet altitude and wouldn't hurt anybody. The dynamite would, however, go off with a hell of a bang and presumably be a psychological blow to the regime.

Simultaneously, Morgan and his immediate followers were to take off for the hills and proclaim a new crusade. In Miami, Pedraza troops, quartered in three sizeable barracks, were to be airlifted to a Morgan-controlled airfield. Another group was to strike from Haiti, a third from the Dominican Republic. Arms were also to be airdropped to the hundreds of Batista soldiers still hiding out in Cuba's many caves.

It is not hindsight to say that I looked at all this feverish activity with blunt skepticism—a skepticism which, it turned out, saved my life.

I didn't trust Morgan. Somehow, it was too pat. Moreover, we were placing all our bets on what was obviously a very unreliable character. I was also shaken by the amateurishness and noisiness of the preparations. General Pedraza himself is quite a man, but his followers and allies were something else again. They turned conspiracy into a circus parade.

But Trujillo was convinced. So was his "prophet," Johnny Abbes, who took over as project officer. The promised $500,000 in cash was turned over to Morgan in Miami, plus another $100,000 thrown in as "expense money." Large sums were sent to Cuban exile groups in Miami. Other big chunks of money were spent in recruiting and transporting an "Anti-Communist Foreign Legion," a force of veteran European mercenaries. Their function was to add a little professional steel to the unstable anti-Castro Cubans.

Two Dominican army radios were smuggled into Cuba

and turned over to Morgan. One was installed in his Havana apartment, the second in a hideout in Las Villas province. Morgan and Abbes communicated in a code worked out by Johnny: they each had an English dictionary and would read off numbers indicating words in the dictionary. They would give the numbers in pairs; first the number of the page, then the number of the word counting from the top—a cumbersome system. Abbes and Morgan soon abandoned it and began shouting at each other over the radio in plain Spanish.

By May, 1959, invasion preparations were so noisy that I was convinced that every Castro agent in the Caribbean must know what was going on.

"General," one of our Miami agents told me, "they're talking about Morgan's counter-revolution in every Cuban bar on Flagler Street." Every day I expected to hear that Castro had tossed Morgan into La Cabana, Castro's fortress-prison.

But nothing happened. Morgan continued to put together an elaborate organization. He seemed to have extensive contacts in the still-powerful sugar growers' and cattlemen's associations. Arms were stockpiled in the hills. The whole Second Front organization appeared to be poised for action.

Then, plans were finalized. Morgan was to seize the seaport of Trinidad in south-central Cuba. He was to knock out communications—roads, highways, bridges—in the area, thus cutting Cuba in half. Pedraza would then move into Trinidad with some 800 exile troops. They would be backed up by about 600 men of the Anti-Communist Legion.

But the strategists had failed to take the State Department into account. Washington had previously winked at the vast flow of contraband arms from Florida to Castro's guerrillas. But there was to be no such immunity for gunrunning to anti-Castro guerrillas. Federal security agencies in the Florida area were heavily reinforced and ordered to block the gunrunning.

Virtually every arms shipment to the Escambray was intercepted, by the U.S., not Castro. (It is interesting to note that, a few months earlier, interception of Castro-bound arms stopped only about ten percent of the total traffic.) Morgan promptly advised Ciudad Trujillo that he wouldn't move unless more munitions reached his men in the Escambray.

Then another disaster threatened. The Cuban government was on the verge of purchasing the eleven Globemasters from the company Morgan had contacted, the Akros Dynamics Company of Cleveland. Akros was preparing to deliver the planes to Cuba. Nelson was badly shaken. If Castro got the planes, Morgan would get his commission. He would also realize that he had been duped into believing the original deal had fallen through. Frank knew that Morgan was perfectly capable of switching sides.

Nelson got in touch with an Akros representative. He tried to persuade the company not to sell the planes. Akros was fairly receptive to Frank's argument. The company was apparently dubious of both the financial and political aspects of the deal. But, said the Akros official, refusal to sell would mean losing a $375,000 sale. Frank thought quickly.

"I think I have a customer for you," he told the Akros man. "I'll see if I can get him to buy a plane for $375,000 so you won't be out any money."

Frank's customer, needless to say, was Trujillo. He listened to Nelson's explanation and nodded. It was a deal.

The Globemaster landed in Miami en route to the Dominican Republic. Trujillo's local gunrunners immediately saw an opportunity. They were losing most of their sea shipments to the federals. Why not use the Globemaster? There were several good reasons why not—the plane was too valuable to use in such a risky operation. Moreover, the gunrunners were inept and under close surveillance by U.S. authorities.

But, unknown to either Akros or Trujillo, the Miami agents tried to ship a load of guns on the Globemaster. Earlier, the Dominican consul in Miami had clumsily attempted to bribe Customs agents into looking the other way. The Customs men took the money, the guns and the Globemaster. The seizure focussed even more attention on our limping "counter-revolution."

Trujillo blew up. The several million dollars allocated to the operation were gone. Other millions were being spent to strengthen and maintain the regular Dominican armed forces and the Foreign Legion. But the Cubans themselves, many of whom had left their country with millions, were contributing damned little. A list of wealthy Cubans was compiled. First name on the list was Fulgencio Batista.

Putting the bite on Batista wasn't easy. Trujillo pressured him for several weeks without success.

Then the Old Man let it be known that he was on the verge of having Batista hauled bodily from his Hotel Jaragua suite and dumped in the sea. Batista suddenly saw the light. An agent was sent to Miami to contact Col. Orlando Piedra, the former Havana chief of police. Orlando, the then-custodian of Batista's funds, was told to turn over one million dollars to the cause. Orlando obeyed. Once again, invasion preparations were pushed.

But Castro struck first. On the afternoon of June 14, 1959, a group of 56 men boarded a C-46 transport plane at Santa Lucia airport near Manzanillo in Cuba's Oriente province. The plane bore Dominican markings.

The men, dressed in olive-green uniforms, were armed with Belgian-made FAL rifles supplied by Fidel. Some men also carried bazookas and machine guns, supplied by the Venezuelan government. The plane itself was also donated by Venezuela.

The plane took off, heading southeast. At the controls sat Cuban air force pilot Orestes Acosta and Juan José Rodriguez, a Venezuelan. In nominal command of the invaders was Enrique Jimenez Moya, former captain in Fidel's army. He had been discharged and made a major in the Dominican Liberation Army.

Military adviser of the group and the real commander was Cuban Maj. Delio Gomez Ochoa. Besides other Cubans and Dominicans, there were Venezuelans, Spaniards, two Guatemalans and two Americans.

Also aboard was a former Dominican Air Force pilot, Capt. Juan de Dios Ventura. A month before, he had defected from the Dominican Republic, flying his jet to Puerto Rico and requesting asylum. The Cuban and Venezuelan governments had immediately taken him over. Ventura's presence with the invaders might inspire other Dominican officers to switch sides.

At dusk that afternoon the plane set down on the airfield of the Dominican town of Constanza, high in the heart of the thinly populated Cordillera Central, and about a hundred miles from Ciudad Trujillo. There was a brief clash with the 15-man local garrison, then the invaders fled into the hills.

They were decimated. Only four survived Trujillo's immediate pursuit.

Two days after the landing, Juan de Dios Ventura, wearing a neat Dominican Air Force uniform with the rank of lieutenant colonel, sat down before the microphones of the government radio station in Cuidad Trujillo. He read a statement:

"I want to state that I am not a traitor. I was sent on a special mission last month by the government. I went to Puerto Rico, Cuba and Venezuela to gather some of these bandits and bring them here to show them that the country is governed by the people and for the people. . . ."

Then Ventura was taken to meet the diplomatic corps.

The U.S. Ambassador—who didn't know who the hell he was—was photographed smilingly shaking hands with Ventura. The picture was used to insinuate that the Ambassador was congratulating Ventura on his feat.

(This was all hokum, of course. Ventura had been no agent; he had been taken prisoner. One of Trujillo's favorite stunts was to capture a revolutionary and give him an alternative; cooperate or die. The prisoner would then go on the air and either beat his breast in remorse or claim to have been a Trujillo agent. This performance would up survival chances from zero to about fifty-fifty.)

But Ventura lost his gamble. Trujillo let him wear his uniform with its new lieutenant-colonel insignia, but kept him under close guard. A month or two after the invasion a Dominican air force plane crashed at sea. Immediately, it was rumored that Ventura had been the pilot and that he had been "accidented." Be that as it may, it was solemnly announced by the press that Ventura had indeed been the pilot of the crashed plane.

Ventura's capture hadn't marked the end of the Castro invasion. On June 18, our agents in Cuba reported that an invasion fleet had left the Cuban port of La Chiva. Simultaneously, Venezuelan ships were maneuvering to divert attention from the real thrust.

But Trujillo was fully aware of what was happening. His spies, some of them involved with Morgan and then including Morgan himself, had carefully followed every move of the invasion force.

Some 600 men had been trained for the invasion at camps in Cuba's Pinar del Rio province. Just prior to embarkation, the bulk of the troops were moved to Oriente province. Troops designated for the sea invasion were sent to Nipe Bay on Cuba's northeast coast.

The three Cuban navy frigates in Nipe Bay, the *José Marti, Maximo Gomez* and *Antonio Maceo,* were ordered to put to sea and head for Great Inagua Island in the Bahamas. The north coast of the Dominican Republic was in easy striking distance from Great Inagua. Most of the troops boarded two yachts, the *Carmen Elsa* and the *Tinina*. The latter ship had belonged to our old friend, enemy and co-conspirator, ex-President Carlos Prio.

The yachts and the warships rendezvoused off Great Inagua. Then all five ships, blacked out, headed in the direction of Puerto Plata on the north coast of the Dominican Republic. Cuban air force planes flew reconnaissance over the area and the pilots reported no sign of military activity.

They were wrong. Not only had Trujillo's spies reported the departure of the invasion force, his communications men were also monitoring the very transmissions which boasted that the invasion would be a big surprise. The ships' communications security was also sloppy as hell. The frigates' radio operators babbled to each other and to Cuba as if they were radio hams on a pleasure cruise.

About ten miles from shore, the frigates put about. The yachts went on in, on their own, and were promptly blasted by bombs and naval gunfire. All died, the peasants helping the troops in the proceedings. There wasn't a sole survivor.

These *campesinos*, incidentally, remained loyal to Trujillo to the end. This revealing little incident took place during the north coast invasion:

A village chief called his men together. "Muchachos," he said, "we have a little job to do," meaning they would have to fight the invaders. "Anybody who doesn't want to fight, step forward."

Two men stepped out. The chief drew his pistol and shot them both through the head. One was his nephew.

One of the few survivors of the airborne invasion was Cuban Maj. Gomez Ochoa. He was taken alive. The slight, blondish Gomez Ochoa can truthfully claim to have come as close to death as any living man.

Gomez Ochoa had died of a "heart attack," in prison, it was officially announced. Then, miraculously, he was restored to life. Acting on a whim, Trujillo had changed his mind at the last moment: Gomez Ochoa could live, at least for a while.

But Gomez Ochoa would have to pay for his continued existence. And pay he did. Again and again, Delio made impassioned public denunciations of Fidel. Again and again, Delio was hauled out of his cell and temporarily installed in a hotel suite so that he could tell foreign correspondents how grateful he was for Trujillo's boundless mercy. That boy really made a production out of it!

His excellent performances were to keep Gomez Ochoa alive until Trujillo's death. A few months later he was released. Delio left the country, denounced the Trujillos, and went home to Fidel. It would be interesting to know what kind of a reception he got.

Hardly had the smoke cleared from the June invasions when attack loomed from another quarter: Puerto Rico. The island had always been a center of anti-Trujillo activity, openly aided by the island government, and reports began to reach Trujillo that a mixed force of Dominican exiles and Puerto Ricans was about to invade.

A still-unexplained event during the following July precipitated quiet but intense diplomatic wrangling. The occurrence, which concerned a shipment of British Army rifles to the Puerto Rican government, never erupted into the open. Each party, for different reasons, preferred to restrict the issue to diplomatic note-passing and intelligence-agentry.

The episode began on July 23, 1959, when the British freighter *Brittany* of the Royal Mail Lines steamed past San Juan's Moro Castle and was warped dockside. The *Brittany* immediately began to discharge her cargo: 120 cases of British .30 cal. military rifles—Enfields—a total of 3,500 to 4,000 rifles. The guns were consigned to the Banco de Fomento (Development Bank) of the Puerto Rican Government.

This was enough in itself to intrigue every intelligence agent in San Juan—U.S. federal, freelance, and foreign— but when additional facts were learned the Enfields became the object of international interest and a near-incident:

1) The consignee was unable to produce an import license for the arms. U.S. customs officials thereupon blocked removal of the guns from the dock.

2) Learning of the federal action, a Fomento official immediately sought reload of arms back on the *Brittany,* for shipment to the freighter's next port of call: La Guaira, Venezuela. The *Brittany* was then casting off, however, and her master apparently refused to delay departure.

3) A spokesman for the Banco de Fomento then asserted that the rifles were to be used for industrial purposes; to be converted into sporting rifles at a Puerto Rican plant.

There was no such conversion plant, however, although it was said that one was planned.

This all was happening at a time when certain Puerto Rican politicians were enthusiastically supporting Fidel Castro and various other revolutionary causes, including the Dominican revolutionary movement.

The Dominican Government viewed the episode as very curious at best, and maybe an attempt to arm the expected invasion. Protests and messages began to fly between Ciudad Trujillo and London, Washington, and San Juan. In the British capital the chief of the American Department of the British Foreign Office promised an immediate investigation of the shipment. Washington shrugged off the suggestion that the Enfields had a purpose more political than sporting. San Juan was silent.

Well, what was the upshot? Frankly, I don't know. The issue dragged on inconclusively for weeks. The last I heard, the United States, Dominican, Puerto Rican and revolutionary agents were all and simultaneously laying watchful siege on that San Juan wharf.

There was, incidentally, another reason for this intense interest: Fidel Castro had also bought a shipment of British Enfields, also to be used as "sporting rifles." And he didn't have a conversion plant either.

Trujillo's attention was shifted back to Cuba on August 5. That was the day Morgan returned from Miami with some $170,000 in cash, extracted both from Trujillo and wealthy Cuban exiles, plus a load of guns. Morgan was either lucky or skillful in slipping through U.S. security with his contraband arms; most of the other shipments were intercepted.

An air of unreality and fantasy permeated the Morgan operation those first two weeks of August, 1959. He and Johnny Abbes had long since thrown away their dictionaries and talked to each other in the clear for hours on end. Morgan demanded immediate action. He talked endlessly, pleading, demanding, giving orders. I listened, fascinated, as Morgan named specific names, places and dates in connection with the landing—all in transmissions which could have been monitored in Helsinki, let alone Havana.

Incessantly, Morgan clamored for more *parque*, more arms and equipment. He gave the Spanish word a curious inflection, cutting short the last syllable, making it sound like "parky." Morgan got his *parque*. He also got ten "invaders." He very nearly got several hundred more, including me.

On August 12, Morgan began to shout into the radio that his men had seized Trinidad. "Trinidad is ours! Don't let us down! We need men, guns, supplies."

By now, Pedraza was suspicious. Even Trujillo was, I think, shaken. Long ago I had come to the conclusion that

Morgan was either mad or a traitor. This view was shared in varying degrees by most participants in our counter-revolution.

But Trujillo dispatched a planeload of munitions to Trinidad. The flight crew climbed out and looked around. In the distance they could hear machine gun fire and explosions. They were greeted by swarms of bearded troops who shouted "Viva Trujillo!" and "Down with Castro!" As we learned later, Fidel himself was standing in the shadows enjoying the scene.

The plane was permitted to return. Trujillo interrogated the crewmen. It sounded like a real revolution, all right. Trujillo decided to greenlight the whole operation.

"Espaillat," Trujillo told me, "you will take command of the forward elements. You will leave for Trinidad tomorrow aboard the first plane."

"But Chief," I protested, "I think this is all a trap. Everything points that way. Castro and Morgan are luring us into a trap."

The Old Man stared at me.

"What's the matter, General, lost your guts?"

"No, Chief, but I haven't seen any blood. I haven't seen any corpses—just words and dramatics, a stageshow. Show me some blood and I will go."

"You'll soon see plenty of blood," the Old Man snapped. He curtly dismissed me.

Trujillo then sent for the American on his staff, gave him the same order, got the same reaction.

"My God," the very shaken American said to me later, "I think he was trying to get me killed off."

That was also my thought. But surely, there were better ways than that.

Fortunately, this include-me-out feeling had become so strong that the "invasion" virtually dissolved, Trujillo notwithstanding.

One plane took off from the Dominican Republic, developed "motor trouble" and returned. Pilots for invasion aircraft in Miami suddenly disappeared. Pedraza's army wasn't prepared to move until the airborne units had established a secure beachhead. In the end, the "invasion" consisted of a lone transport plane. With ten men aboard, it landed where Morgan had designated and was greeted by Fidel Castro and 3,000 troops.

But there were hundreds of us who just missed making our television debuts when Castro paraded his captives before TV cameras. All those radio conversations between Morgan and Abbes were also re-broadcast. Castro had had them taped. And Alex Hernandez, a key figure in the Miami end of the conspiracy, turned up back in Havana to add to the general merriment. He had been a Castro agent.

Trujillo must have been mortified by the debacle, but he didn't show it. Nor did I dare let slip any I-told-you-so remarks. That would have been suicide. Miraculously, Johnny Abbes survived the fiasco. It had been taken for granted that he would be "accidented." I think the Old Man was just so embarrassed that he wanted to forget about the whole thing.

For Fidel, the Morgan operation was a double triumph. He had managed to bring off an "invasion" of Cuba just as the inter-American foreign ministers conference was getting underway in Santiago de Chile. But far more important, the plot enabled Castro to break the back of his internal opposition.

Powerful groups within Cuba were attempting to organize to resist the agrarian reform program. The Second Front of the Escambray was basically hostile to the regime. The strongest open resistance Castro ever faced was in the summer and fall of 1959.

Altogether, about 6,000 people were arrested in connection with the Morgan conspiracy. Among those Morgan betrayed to Castro were some 2,000 members of his own

Second Front organization. Others were merely opponents of agrarian reform. It was never clear how many of the latter had actually been lured into the conspiracy.

In any event, the Morgan incident terminated in the collapse of all open opposition to the regime. Castro had no trouble in squelching isolated outbursts of rebellion which flared during the following October.

It is futile to speculate whether Morgan's plot was a Castro conspiracy from the beginning. People who worked with him are convinced that Morgan began with sincere intentions. They believe that the plot was discovered in May or June and Morgan was forced to follow through as a Castro agent. In any event, Morgan was eventually put before a firing squad. That ending was as certain as Morgan's tendency to shift in any direction which seemed in his best interests.

Trujillo never quite recovered from the fiasco. It was his Bay of Pigs and, like the U.S. government, he lost much of his enthusiasm for cloak-and-dagger operations against Castro. I think it shook his confidence in himself. I know that his lieutenants began to wonder whether the Old Man was slipping. He seemed to have lost touch with reality.

The Cuban exiles themselves also helped dampen Trujillo's anti-Castro ardor. The various groups and their leaders feuded constantly with each other. The money he spent supporting them was wasted. He also became weary of Washington's constant harassment of his anti-Castro activities. Finally, he ran all the Cuban refugees out of the country.

The Old Man finally decided to settle the Castro problem in a typically Trujillo fashion: he would have him assassinated. I really think that Fidel would be dead today if the plot had not been called off.

An American once close to Castro had secured an apartment within sight of CMQ in Havana, the television studios where Fidel makes his broadcasts. Firing from the apartment window, a crack shot could put a bullet through Fidel as he entered or left the studio. And the American was an expert rifleman.

It was a natural. Trujillo agreed to pay the American one million dollars for a bullet driven through Fidel's bearded head.

The only problem was modification of a rifle which would meet the American's requirements. He wanted a sniper's rifle, equipped with special telescopic sights and silencer. Dominican ordnance experts went to work to produce the rifle.

The weapon was completed and was en route to Cuba when Trujillo cancelled the project. He had good reason.

The pressure from Washington had mounted to the point of open hostility. The Old Man suddenly realized that, by reverse logic, U.S. government officials had convinced themselves that Trujillo was as much a threat as Castro. Knock off Fidel and the full weight of Washington's fury and frustration would fall on Trujillo. Better that the pressure be shared by two targets instead of one. The U.S. government had become his most dangerous foe.

I think Trujillo now knew for the first time that he could not resist indefinitely. But I know that he was resolved to go down fighting. All the dictators who had sought sanctuary in the Dominican Republic had one thing in common: they had fled "to avoid further bloodshed." That was not Trujillo's way.

"Whoever begins a revolt against me," Trujillo snarled as he retreated into isolation, "theirs will be the blame for the bloodshed and theirs the blood that will be shed."

The prediction proved partly correct: the blood of conspirators did flow, but his did as well.

15

Operation Galindez

And so Trujillo fell. But for me, it was only the beginning—the beginning of a new life as exile, author and object of intense interest by a half dozen intelligence agencies. I find this new career as interesting as the old. I am under constant surveillance, my telephone is tapped—and very sloppily, I must say—and I am periodically honored by the visits of agents representing various governments and governmental departments. Periodically, too, pressure is brought to bear to have me deported from whatever country I am in. Yes, it is an interesting life.

Why all the fuss? Well, I'll have to use that cliché about "the man who knew too much." Some people are distinctly upset about my willingness to speak out on such sticky topics as the assassination of Trujillo and his bribery of Washington politicians. Another reason is that some day my presence in some country near the U.S. might re-awaken interest in the Galindez case. That is quite a story.

On the evening of March 12, 1956, a middle-aged Basque exile named Jesus de Galindez boarded a Manhattan subway and was never seen again. Trujillo was immediately accused of having him kidnapped, and thereby was set in motion the first of the series of events which culminated in his death and the destruction of his dictatorship. The tensions generated by the Galindez affair were summed up by reporter Milton Bracker in *The New York Times* of September 2, 1957:

163

"MYSTERIES STRAIN
U.S.-DOMINICAN TIE
UNSOLVED GALINDEZ-MURPHY
CASES DISTURB DIPLOMATIC
AND BUSINESS RELATIONS

by Milton Bracker

"Both the State Department and the Department of Justice are engaged in a ceaseless effort to answer two questions:

"What happened to Dr. Jesus de Galindez, Basque representative and Columbia University instructor, in New York on March 12, 1956?

"What happened to Gerald Lester Murphy, Oregonian employed as a pilot by the Dominican Republic's commercial airline in Ciudad Trujillo, on Dec. 3, 1956?

"The double mystery has seriously strained relations between the United States and the Dominican Republic. This strain is a source of embarrassment to American businessmen with long-range ventures in the Caribbean country. These include a former Assistant Secretary of State and a former Ambassador.

"The case has also provoked bitter exchanges between the Dominican Republic and Puerto Rico. The President of the Dominican Congress has sharply criticized Gov. Luis Munoz Marin of Puerto Rico. Luis Munoz Lee, a son of the Governor, publishes an English-language weekly in San Juan that has been notably sympathetic to Dominican exiles there.

IMPULSE TO INVESTIGATION

"Moreover, the case has impelled Generalissimo Rafael Leonidas Trujillo, Dominican dictator, to subsidize an inquiry of his own. It is underway at 515 Madison Avenue, and will eventually move to the Dominican capital. The investigators are Morris L. Ernst, attorney long identified with liberal causes, and former State Supreme Court Justice William H. Munson.

"At the same time, the furor has caused the dictator to pour more thousands of dollars into various public relations efforts. One aim is to counteract a 6½ per cent drop in tourist arrivals in the Dominican Republic for the first seven months of this year.

"Dr. Galindez, born in Madrid in 1915, had lived in the Dominican Republic for six years. He was known to have completed the manuscript of a book, since published in Chile, that was critical of Generalissimo Trujillo. . . ."

Mr. Bracker then made an heroic effort to cut his way editorially through the jungle of charges and countercharges concerning the Galindez case. It wasn't easy. Nor did Mr. Bracker entirely succeed in making clear why my name "has figured repeatedly" in the investigations. He wrote:

"General Espaillat, not yet 36, was a member of the class of '43 at West Point. On the day of Dr. Galindez's disappearance, he was in Ciudad Trujillo, serving as Under Secretary of Defense. Not quite seven weeks later, he came to New York as consul general and alternate representative at the United Nations. After several trips back and forth, he returned to his homeland, where last July 1 he became Minister of State Security.

"General Espaillat is a tall, slim, loose-jointed man with a thin, wide moustache. He has declared formally that the idea that the Dominicans had 'snatched' a man from the streets of New York was preposterous.

THE EXCHANGE OF NOTES

"The Trujillo Government has said General Espaillat would be available to questioning by any United States

authorities—but in his own country and without a waiver
of immunity.

"The latest note in the curious diplomatic exchange came
from the Dominicans on June 24. It was not made public
textually, but is understood not to have altered Generalissimo Trujillo's stand.

"What, if anything, the FBI has established beyond
the generally known facts has not been revealed. The recently accredited United States Ambassador to the Dominican Republic, Joseph Farland, himself had two years of
experience as an FBI agent. In New York, the FBI has
been known to send a man within minutes of hearing of a
conversation in which a Dominican was quoted as having
described the Galindez case as an 'accident.'

"All of this adds up to an air of doubts and distrust that
has put Washington's dealings with Generalissimo Trujillo
on an uneasy plane. Yet the evidence against the dictator
remains circumstantial.

"Influential and respected Americans continue to praise
Generalissimo Trujillo and to do business with him."

As Bracker indicated, I have been a favorite suspect—
if only for public consumption—in the case. However, let
me make one thing clear: this is no attempt "to clear my
name" nor an "appeal for justice." I don't care about that.
I do resent, however, having been used as a fall guy for
other people's stupidity and mistakes. I think it would be
a splendid idea to hold a really objective investigation of
the Galindez case, but you may be sure that will never be
done.

First of all, the real facts behind the case have been well
suppressed. Only now and again do some of those facts
surface, as in a Drew Pearson column shortly after the Bay
of Pigs fiasco.

EASY COME, SECRET GO
MONEY'S NO OBJECT TO THE CIA
by Drew Pearson

"One aspect of the Central Intelligence Agency which few people realize is that it is the only government agency which does not have to submit its expenses to an accounting. Its books are not scrutinized by the General Accounting Office, and the congressional appropriations committees do not make the agency justify its funds, as with other branches of government.

"This makes for reckless, irresponsible spending, sometimes by Ivy Leaguers who have had little experience in hiring ships, buying arms, and masterminding political revolutions, as in Cuba.

"It also tends to make the CIA representative in foreign capitals more important than the American Ambassador. The CIA has an unlimited bankroll, the ambassador's expenses are carefully restricted.

"The man with the money usually has the greatest influence, and word soon gets around in most capitals that the man to talk to is not the American Ambassador but the CIA man. . . .

"CIA inefficiency and extravagance in regard to the Cuban invasion might be condoned on the ground of expediency, if the invasion had been successful, or if CIA had not been caught in weird expeditures in the past.

"One of the weirdest was the tremendous sums of money the CIA gave Prof. Jesus de Galindez of Columbia University, who was kidnapped March 12, 1956, while entering a New York subway and has never been heard of since.

"His disappearance has generally been attributed to Dictator Trujillo of the Dominican Republic.

"Beyond any question of doubt, Professor Galindez was being paid by Central Intelligence, even though he was head of the Spanish Basque resistance movement in North and South America, working to overthrow Generalissimo Franco in Spain.

"The official policy of the United States Government, whether right or wrong, has been to support Franco. We have naval and air bases in Spain. We have spent over two billion dollars building these bases and supporting Franco. Yet Central Intelligence spent around $1,000,000 supporting the man who was trying to overthrow Franco.

"Monthly installments were paid to Professor Galindez by the CIA ranging from $4,845 in March 1950 to $26,039 in January 1956, just before Galindez was disposed of. During the years between 1950 and 1956, this mysterious college professor, an exile from Spain, received either $1,016,-000 according to Justice Department files, or $762,527 according to a New York City audit.

"Immediately after Galindez disappeared, Allen Dulles, head of Central Intelligence, phoned New York city officials with an urgent request that a CIA agent be permitted to go through Galindez's papers. This was done. And the last incriminating CIA check, for $7,240 in February, was taken out of the file.

"The mystery remains unsolved as to why CIA was financing a Spanish Basque exile who was working against the government leader we were supporting with military and foreign aid.

"Thus taxpayers were put in the position of both paying to support Franco and paying to undermine Franco.

"It indicates the mysterious operation of Central Intelligence, the agency which may be entirely necessary in these days of the cold war, but which should be kept under some kind of supervision by Congress and the General Accounting Office."

Actually, there was even more to the case than the fact that Galindez was an anti-Franco agent of the Central Intelligence Agency. As a veteran Caribbean intelligence officer—with contacts in every Central American country— I can state with some authority that the disappearance of Jesus de Galindez produced a chain reaction which eventually was a factor in permitting the Communist capture of Cuba.

You may recall the powerful publicity barrages against Trujillo during 1956 and 1957. Newspapers, magazines, television networks, pressure groups and U.S. officials used the case as a club to bash Trujillo. Trujillo had done in Galindez and that was that. Seventeen distinct versions— I counted them—of how it was done were offered in proof.

And, beginning in 1957, the range of the continuing publicity bombardment began to expand. All Latin American dictators began to come under fire, not just Trujillo. In the wave of unrest beginning to sweep Latin America, the publicists drew clear lines between the "bad guys"—the Latin strongmen—and the "good guys"—the aspiring or real Fidel Castros. In the U.S., there came to be uncritical acceptance of this two dimensional formula, that the only acceptable alternative to a Batista was a Castro.

Such was the ultimate impact of the Galindez case, and the centers of public opinion in the U.S. watched passively while Castro entrenched himself in Cuba. Even though Castro's pro-Communist past was a matter of record, he "was the only alternative."

Trujillo probably only added to the confusion by simultaneously spending huge sums of money in the States to defend himself. I would estimate that Trujillo spent between five and ten million dollars on bribes and "public relations." Trujillo's Washington agents threw money around like confetti.

The following incident will give you some idea of the sums involved:

Trujillo sent an aide, Col. Ernesto Vega Pagan, to the States in 1958 with a suitcase stuffed with one million dollars in one hundred-dollar bills. Unfortunately, Vega Pagan had neglected to get a diplomatic visa for his diplomatic passport. So when Pagan's plane landed in the U.S., Customs officials told the colonel that he would have to submit to routine customs inspection. Vega Pagan was understandably shaken at the prospect.

Clutching his suitcase, Vega Pagan put through a frantic phone call to Trujillo. What should he do now?

The situation struck Trujillo as being very funny indeed. He roared with laughter. "Don't worry," he told Vega Pagan. "There are people in Washington who are extremely interested in getting that suitcase through unopened. Just sit tight."

Trujillo then called Manuel de Moya, Dominican Ambassador to Washington, and explained the situation. Get some of your high-priced friends moving on this, Trujillo told de Moya. Vega Pagan told me later that somebody telephoned the Customs office. And Vega Pagan was then immediately extended every courtesy and went on his way, the million dollars uninspected.

What did Trujillo get for his money? Nothing much— an occasional puff piece by some obliging American publication, meaningless words of praise by a number of prominent church and political leaders. In short, Trujillo bought words.

The amount of verbiage Trujillo hurled at the American public was prodigious. Pro-Trujillo propaganda was published as paid advertisements in various U.S. publications. Sometimes the publications would reap enough ads to turn out a "special edition" devoted to praising the Era of Trujillo. The Old Man's press agents in New York and Washington churned out reams of uninspired prose, later to be mouthed by U.S. public figures. Trujillo lobbyists contacted Congressmen by the score. The pros and cons of Generalissimo Trujillo were hotly debated on the floor of Congress.

Following are extracts from a few typical speeches made in connection with the Galindez hassle:

On May 8, 1957, Congressman John McCormack, then House majority leader (and now Speaker of the House), inserted some remarks in the Congressional Record. He noted that four Jewish members of the House had just returned from a Jewish refugee colony in the Dominican Republic and gave a glowing account of what they had seen. Congressman McCormack continued:

"Mr. Speaker, it is encouraging to note that four of my distinguished colleagues, in the course of a visit to the Dominican Republic, formed the same favorable impression of the broad, humanitarian policies of Generalissimo Rafael Leonidas Trujillo Molina, L.L.D., that have been entertained by numerous United States leaders and citizens throughout the last 27 years."

George S. Long, Congressman from Louisiana, was equally ecstatic:

"It has been widely and loosely said that the Dominican Republic is a dictatorship. . . . I have learned not to be taken in by the word 'dictator'. . . . If indeed the Dominican Republic is a dictatorship, we have no proof of the fact that would stand up under a court of law of our nation. . . . The Dominican Republic and its chief of the armed forces [Rafael Trujillo] . . . and its President [brother Hector] . . . have always and unequivocally been on the side of God and Christianity."

On one day alone, July 19, 1957, Trujillo was defended in the House of Congress by Congressmen Donald L. Jackson, Pat Hillings, James G. Fulton, Daniel J. Flood, Victor Anfuso, Abraham Multer, Barratt O'Hara, Clement Zablocki and others. This went on for several years. But all the nice speeches failed to stop "Operation Galindez," as Trujillo's publicists called it.

Trujillo made one last major effort in 1958. He agreed when his Washington agent, Frank Rosenbaum, proposed that New York attorney Morris L. Ernst and publicist Sydney S. Baron be retained to investigate the case. Baron would publicize Ernst's findings. Many thousands of dollars again changed hands.

When Ernst's investigators went to work, one very odd aspect of the case became immediately apparent: despite all the sound and fury, no one had uncovered, or at least not reported, facts which were readily available. *It took no Sherlock Holmes to discover at once that CIA had entered the case as soon as Galindez disappeared.*

As mentioned earlier, CIA officials were given permission to go through Galindez's papers and remove certain documents: not only the check issued by the CIA to Galindez, but also a ledger in Galindez's handwriting.

At this point, Dulles promptly re-entered the case. The CIA chief called Ernst to Washington and told him that exposure of Galindez's anti-Franco role and the source and destination of the funds would "imperil the lives of 200 to 400 people."

So Ernst agreed to withhold this and other explosive evidence which he had since uncovered. It was his understanding that the affair would be clarified at some vague future date.

Later Ernst regretted his decision. He issued a watered-down, truncated version of his findings in a report released in July, 1958. It was bitterly attacked by powerful groups and individuals committed to the Trujillo-kidnapped-Galindez theory. Ernst's personal integrity was smeared. Washington officials stubbornly refused to clarify the case despite Ernst's agreement to censor his report.

The Justice Department concluded an elaborate investigation of the case, but refused to disclose its findings. A congressional move to investigate the source and destination of Galindez's mysterious million was quashed.

Curiously, the American Civil Liberties Union, loudest of the Trujillo-kidnapped-Galindez groups, then abruptly reversed its stand: the ACLU issued a strong statement opposing any Congressional probing of Galindez's disappearance, although for months previously the ACLU had tirelessly demanded investigation of the Dominican "network of terror" which it claimed had kidnapped Galindez.

Government agencies, pressure groups and the directors of several mass communication mediums—all committed to the original theory—combined to suppress any further reference to the Galindez case: Trujillo kidnapped Galindez and that was that.

Surprised and angry, Ernst wrote a letter to Baron requesting that he be authorized to re-open the case. In his letter, dated August 12, 1958, Ernst wrote:

"Friends of mine in Washington have brought me reports which indicate that our government would like nothing better than to put the Galindez case to sleep. . . . I write to you because I am convinced that the case cannot be put to rest as long as our government is suppressing the truth. In fact, the policy is now made in part by *The New York Times, Life* magazine and CBS, which for a long time had been deeply committed to attach the case to your client. . . .

"Although the CIA saw a draft of my original report, I will in the supplement feel perfectly free to refer to my relations to government agencies and the cooperation of the CIA, and print if necessary most of the copies of the Galindez letters which point with clarity to the nature of the operation and the code used in Spain. I will not hesitate to refer to the Galindez ledger, the Zanetti mystery, the disappearance of unreported Galindez moneys, etc. In retrospect, I probably was too decent, believing that Part V of my report, which indicated the kind of material I possessed, would have some public effect on the State Department and the Department of Justice, so that the false accusation regarding the Galindez disappearance would be corrected.

"You may recall that I did not go to the CIA," Ernst continued, "it sent for me. It sent for me I assume because it realized that I had gotten into my possession knowledge indicating that the Galindez mystery must derive from the story of his million dollars and his acting as a double agent in relation to the future of Spain after the death of Franco. CIA admitted to me its relation to Galindez and you know the pressure it used to hide the moneys received between Jan. 30 (1956) and March 12, the date of his disappearance."

Ernst was referring to the check for $7,240 which the CIA had sent to Galindez in February and which was recovered by CIA agents. Ernst suspected that other checks had also been secreted. He found evidence indicating that Galindez had received far larger sums than the $1,016,000 he had reported.

"Whether Galindez was put underground or killed by the Communists or the CIA, I do not know," Ernst admitted. "He may have been killed, but he may have been allowed to go underground for fear that he has left documentation with some friends which would be dynamite if exposed on his death."

Galindez was obviously dynamite, alive or dead. Ernst proposed that he be given authority to release the uncensored version on September 5, 1958. He wanted no additional payment, he said. He was angry at the conspiracy of silence which prevented refutation of the original Galindez theory.

"No government should behave in this ignoble fashion," Ernst wrote Baron, "and if it does so behave it is no longer a free agent since our government of necessity reacts in relation to the important mass media.

"I well understand the desire of your client to submit to the pressure of our government to forget the entire affair. Fortunately or unfortunately, my retainer indicated that it was my duty to report the truth and your duty to disseminate it. . . ."

Nevertheless, Ernst did not release the full report. Trujillo replied that he had no desire to rehash the case. He had spent huge sums in efforts to clear his name and they had come to nothing. He washed his hands, he said, of the whole affair. While this decision was prompted in part by Trujillo's characteristically Latin fatalism, it was also largely based on the advice of William Pawley, a close friend. Pawley felt that the harm had already been done, that continual involvement in the Galindez case would merely add to the damage.

But the State Department was determined that Trujillo would continue to be involved, and that *I* was the best point of attack! The newspapers cooperated enthusiastically. I had been named Dominican Consul General in New York on May 1, six weeks after Galindez disappeared; nevertheless, the press invariably referred to me as having been Consul General in New York when he vanished.

Eventually, a man was produced who claimed he had seen me at a New York airport renting a plane. This was most extraordinary, since I was in the Dominican Republic at the time, escorting Cardinal de la Torre of Ecuador. The Cardinal was attending the Catholic Congress for World Peace then underway in Santo Domingo. Furthermore, a picture of myself and the cardinal had appeared on that date in the newspapers.

No one showed any inclination to check with the Cardinal, much less interrogate a Prince of the Church. But that didn't stop the State Department from demanding that I be removed from my new post of Secretary of Security and be returned to the States for questioning. The demand was virtually unprecedented, of course, and State must have known perfectly well that it would be impossible for any government to humble itself in that manner. However, it did make for good anti-Trujillo publicity.

A compromise was offered. I would go to the U.S. Embassy in the Dominican Republic, and U.S. federal agents could question me at their leisure. The offer was rejected. I suppose there wasn't any publicity mileage in that!

As time passed, it became increasingly apparent that

there were three distinct policies within the U.S. government regarding me and the Galindez case. The State Department saw the issue as a useful weapon against Trujillo —but one with a two-edged blade; and State was careful that the case did not get out of control.

CIA—and I was in almost constant contact with CIA officials concerning Latin American intelligence matters— obviously wished that they had never heard of Jesus de Galindez. They wanted no part of the continuing publicity.

As for the FBI, it became apparent that the Bureau had been drawn into the case without knowing its real national and international ramifications. Time and again, FBI agents have interrogated people about matters which would be already known to the State Department or CIA. It was really amazing. It was as if the different agencies worked for different governments!

Several times since Trujillo's death I have volunteered to come to the United States and submit to questioning. Once I wrote to Gen. Maxwell Taylor, as a fellow West Pointer, offering to make the trip. Gen. Taylor acknowledged my letter but no visa was forthcoming.

On another occasion I contacted the Miami office of the FBI and offered to place myself at their disposal. I was in exile in Nassau at that time. But before the FBI could act, pressure was brought to bear on the Bahamian government and I was deported. One Bahamian official stated, in so many words, that State Department pressure was responsible.

This sort of thing has now happened so many times that it is obvious that some people in Washington not only don't want to investigate the Galindez case, but are also even allergic to my being even close to the United States. They hope, I suppose, that I will go off to Spain or some equally remote place, and then quietly drop out of sight.

Epilogue

LIFE in exile has not been dull. I went first to Nassau in the Bahamas. That didn't last long. The State Department applied pressure and I was given 48 hours to get out. Then I went to Jamaica. The State Department's response was even speedier. I was given 24 hours to leave.

Next it was Curacao—with an entourage of Washington agents right behind me. But I had friends in Curacao. The chief inspector of police, an old friend, assigned one of his top officers to try to help me keep the Washington agents off my back.

"There is one place where you may be able to hide out," my friend told me. "That's the island of St. Martin." So we went to St. Martin.

That was the beginning of a hilarious two-week comedy. St. Martin is a tiny, remote island that is owned half by the Dutch and half by the French. Total population is no more than three or four thousand. When I arrived, that sleepy little island suddenly saw more activity than it had experienced in years.

The local Dutch police chief was delighted with my arrival. It's tough to be a policeman when there isn't anything much to police. So we had a party. Our little fiesta lasted for a couple of days, then was interrupted by the arrival of my Washington entourage. And the word was passed to the Dutch administrator: Espaillat has to go.

And Espaillat went—to the French half of the island. The Curacao police inspector and I acquired a battered little Renault, loaded it with booze, and chugged down the single road which joins the two sectors. The French police chief was even happier to see us than his Dutch counterpart. And could he put away the cognac!

Well, my entourage promptly shifted to the French end of the island and passed the same word. Espaillat had to go. Espaillat went. Back down the road to Dutch territory. The Washington agents returned and again lodged a formal protest. The Dutch administrator could point out that I had indeed left. I was "asked" to leave again. So I went back to French territory. So did my tireless entourage.

It probably could have gone on indefinitely. Sometimes I was "asked" to leave twice a day, always to be met by bottles of cognac and gin thrust upon me by one or the other of the two police chiefs. But I was beginning to feel like a ping-pong ball and the alcoholic content of my body had reached the saturation point. I left.

Canada was next. I landed at Ottawa in September, 1961. This move apparently caught my Washington friends by surprise. I was admitted without hesitation. However, when I applied for residence some months later the old process began anew. My application was rejected on technical reasons which are ignored in the vast majority of cases. Deportation proceedings began anew.

At this writing, my case is before the Supreme Court. What the upshot will be, I have no idea. My future seems to depend on what I say, or don't say, about Trujillo's payoffs to Washington politicians.

Here, for instance, is a notation made by my lawyer, Mr. Charles Sirois:

"June 29th, 1962, received telephone call from Mr. Espaillat. He says that Sgt. Stewart of the Royal Canadian Mounted Police and Allen, his assistant, went to his home June 28 and said they wanted to question him in order to reassure themselves that no Canadians were involved in any dirty work in the Dominican Republic before and after

Trujillo's death. At RCMP headquarters, Charles Lyons of the Security Division of the State Department of the U.S.A., in front of Stewart and Allen, with the consent of Espaillat, questioned him as to whether he knew anything about U.S. Congressmen involved in payola by Trujillo.

"During the interview, Lyons, after insisting that he did not influence the Canadian authorities re Espaillat's application for immigration, said: 'Prove your good faith and give us the information re payola by Trujillo to U.S. Congressmen and we will put a good word on your behalf with the Canadian authorities.'"

I told Mr. Lyons to put his good word in first and then I would sing like Trujillo's birds. We got nowhere. Mr. Lyons apparently wanted only to determine how much I knew.

As I said before, there is sometimes a startling lack of coordination between different bureaus of the U.S. government, a flaw which is probably unavoidable in huge governments. I was again struck by this when I talked to a team of FBI men a month or so after Mr. Lyons' visit. As before, the two-day interview was held at RCMP headquarters in the presence of Canadian security officers.

We went through the same routine as before. It was obvious that the U.S. government was conducting two completely separate investigations. Moreover, it was equally plain that the FBI and the State Department tend to view each other with mutual suspicion.

Both their investigations are global in scope; I have friends, relatives and former associates in a dozen countries who have been questioned by Justice and/or State Department agents. Only rarely do the results of the many interrogations emerge into public view. The investigations are quiet but feverish. This situation was well-expressed in an article by Robert Jones which appeared in *The Indianapolis Star* of January 22, 1963:

"A shadowy but explosive drama is being enacted be-

hind the scenes in Washington these days. If a fraction of
the whispered reports are true, a situation may be in the
making which could explode with a far bigger bang than
the Teapot Dome scandal of the '20's.

"A swarm of government investigators are feverishly
searching for the answer to this question:

"Was the late Dictator Rafael Trujillo of the Dominican
Republic making payoffs to a number of key United States
congressmen, diplomats, journalists and even a one-time
candidate for the nomination for the presidency of the
U.S.?

"This question has been put to scores of Dominicans and
Americans who had some connection with the assassinated
strongman.

"And many have answered in the affirmative.

"Now under way is a frantic hunt of proof of the
charges. No one, apparently, is sure what will be done if
that proof is obtained. Important figures in both major political parties, it is said, may be involved.

"The search for evidence centers about the alleged existence of secret files which are reported to document the
payoffs to prominent Americans. Those files are supposed
to have been spirited out of the Dominican Republic and
are believed to be in Washington.

"At this point, the investigation becomes even more
weird.

"The evidence is believed to be in the hands of certain
officials of the U.S. government—but which officials not
even the investigators seem to know.

"It is a definite fact that Federal investigators are trying
to identify the Federal officials who might have had access
to the Trujillo files in the Dominican Republic. Witnesses
have been queried about the probable location of those
files in Washington. Answers have ranged from the Department of Agriculture to the White House. . . .

"*Ugliest aspect of the investigation is the evident fear*

*that the alleged bribe-takers will be politically blackmailed
by the officials or bureaus possessing the proof. It is feared
that threat of exposure would force vulnerable politicians
into a sort of political slavery.*

*"If this is even partly true, it is not too much to say that
the upshot of this investigation may change the course of
U.S. history. But it is equally possible that the whole affair
will be safely buried."*

From the investigators' questions, it is easy to pinpoint
the people the FBI believes might know something about
Trujillo's American activities. They are Manuel de Moya,
former Dominican ambassador to Washington (and his
former assistants, Claudio Saillant, Jorge Rodriguez and
Adalgisa Nicolas); playboy-diplomat Porfirio Rubirosa;
former figurehead Presidents Hector Trujillo and Joaquin
Balaguer; ex-Col. Ernesto Vega Pagan; Trujillo's former
interpreter, Otto Vega; Tirso Rivera, Trujillo's financial
secretary; former diplomats Luis Mercado and Luis
Oviedo.

The Americans, Trujillo's financial advisors, millionaire-
socialite Herbert May and lawyer Frank Rosenbaum; lobbyists James Donohue and Michael B. Deane; society columnist Igor Cassini (Cholly Knickerbocker); Joseph G.
Feeney, White House aide during the Truman administration; General George Olmstead; officials of several Washington law firms; assorted minor characters; and the administrative assistants or five or six Congressmen.

As *The Indianapolis Star* indicated, much of the FBI's
questioning centers about the location of the files docu-
menting the payola. The investigators know that the files
were turned over to U.S. officials by the interim Dominican
government—the regime at that time was virtually an ap-
pendage of the State Department—but the documents then
apparently disappeared from sight.

They almost came to the surface in Senator Fulbright's
recent investigation of the activities of "the sugar lobby,"

and some of the material reached public view in a *Saturday Evening Post* article dealing with Igor Cassini. That this information, which could be the death blow to many a public servant, has been suppressed, may give some idea of the powerful persons involved.

Again and again these questions are put to former Trujillo officials.

"Do you know the names of the American diplomats who secured the files?"

"What U.S. officials had enough influence with the post-Trujillo Dominican government to secure the files?"

"Do you have any idea where the files are now?"

"If they are in Washington, what officials do you think have them?"

"*The New York Times* has printed confidential correspondence from Trujillo's files. Whom do you think leaked that material to the *Times?*"

And so on. Samples of other questions:

"Is it true that Trujillo contributed to the 1956 presidential campaign and that there is a letter from the national committee of one of the two major American political parties acknowledging that donation?"

"What was the amount of the donation? To whom was it paid?"

"What did Trujillo get for his money?"

"How were the pay-offs made?"

"What are the names of Trujillo's Washington agents?"

"Can you remember specific dates when payments were made, by whom, to whom and how much?"

"What specific services did these politicians perform for Trujillo?"

"Where is the list of code names of the politicians receiving pay-offs, the so-called 'Paula list'?"

"We have reason to suspect that Trujillo was paying $2,000 a month to the Caribbean bureau chief of a major American news agency. Is that true?"

"Did the American Embassy in the Dominican Republic know about the payola?"

Then there are the questions relating specifically to the federal indictment against Igor Cassini, the New York society columnist who also runs a public relations agency. There is no doubt that Trujillo and his staff considered Cassini to be our agent. He was hired because he was a friend of the Kennedys and other powerful financial-political figures.

However, people being interviewed sometimes put this question to the investigators: why was Cassini, who is a relative minnow, selected for indictment when there are political whales who could be harpooned? No clear answer is given.

As for myself, who helped get the bribery pot boiling, I will joyfully attempt to keep stirring it. You may be sure that this is one old soldier who won't just fade away.

Ottawa, Canada
September, 1963

Index

185